Taking Inquiry to Scale

NCTE Editorial Board

Taking Inquiry to Scale

An Alternative to Traditional Approaches to Education Reform

Michael J. Palmisano

NATIONAL COUNCIL OF TEACHERS OF ENGLISH
1111 W. KENYON ROAD, URBANA, ILLINOIS 61801-1096

National Council of
Teachers of English

NCLE NATIONAL CENTER FOR
LITERACY EDUCATION

Staff Editor: Bonny Graham
Interior Design: Jenny Jensen Greenleaf
Cover Design: Pat Mayer
Cover Image: Donald W. Fonner

NCTE Stock Number: 49942

Library of Congress Cataloging-in-Publication Data

Palmisano, Michael J., 1947–
    Taking inquiry to scale : an alternative to traditional approaches to education reform / Michael J. Palmisano.
        pages cm
    Includes bibliographical references and index.
    ISBN 978-0-8141-4994-2 (pbk.)
    1. School improvement programs—United States. 2. Educational change—United States. 3. Teachers—Training of—United States. 4. Group work in education—United States. 5. Team learning approach in education—United States. I. Title.
    LB2822.82.P34 2013
    371.2'07—dc23
                                                                2013006384

For my grandchildren
Gianna, Charlie, and Luca
True North.

Contents

Preface

I have served in several educator roles. I began my career as a middle and then elementary school teacher, assistant principal, and learning center director. As a graduate student, I became increasingly interested in the district's role in supporting learning and teaching. I served in leadership roles in several school districts, with responsibilities for curriculum, instruction, program evaluation, and professional development. I spent the last decade of my years in public education as an administrator at the Illinois Mathematics and Science Academy (IMSA), Illinois's residential high school for gifted students in mathematics and science. While at IMSA, I served in leadership roles focused on the academy's internal program for students and on external professional development and student programs. During this time, I was invited by the Illinois State Board of Education to cochair Illinois's Learning Standards Project, where I witnessed education policy, practice, research, and politics come together.

When I left the academy, I worked with regional school accreditation associations, where I developed materials to support school and school district improvement and accreditation. In 2004 I was invited to join the Board of Directors of the Ball Foundation, a family-funded and operating foundation established in 1975 and based in Glen Ellyn, Illinois. Through its commitment to discovering and developing human potential, the Ball Foundation partners with midsize urban school districts using a system-wide learning and change approach to increase literacy achievement for all students. As I joined the Foundation board, the Education Initiatives (EI) team was supporting long-term school district partnerships in California, Illinois, and Michigan.

It was an exciting time for the EI team because it was embarking on a new generation of school district partnerships. Intrigued by the approach the EI team was taking, I accepted an invitation from Bob Hill, director of EI, to join the team and step into what the EI team saw as an action research project to bring about and learn from a whole system change through a systems learning alternative to traditional approaches to education reform. Together we committed to working systemically, adaptively, and in inquiry-based ways to improve instruction, leadership, and organizational practices to ensure literacy achievement for all students.

For the next five years, we supported a partnership with a midsize urban school district in Southern California where significant numbers of students come from impoverished backgrounds, English is not the language spoken at home, and White students are the minority. As the work unfolded, I was drawn to the tension, sometimes creative and always difficult, between the content and the process dimensions of our partnership work. Attending to *content* (instruction and leadership practice and underlying organizational conditions that affect teaching and learning) while attending to *process* (bringing together educators from across the district in learning with and from one another) was a persistent challenge. At the same time, our team learning was most exciting and enlightening when we worked at the nexus of content and process. All of this unfolded as the school district experienced massive budget cuts, reorganization, shifting student demographics, and mounting pressures to meet No Child Left Behind Act accountability requirements.

As our partnership evolved, my interest in the systemic and inquiry dimensions of our work grew as well. I wrestled with such questions as: *What does it really mean to take education reform to scale? What is there about inquiry-based professional learning that contributes to student results? How can a school district support system-wide professional inquiry? Can collaborative inquiry be a scalable alternative to traditional approaches to education reform?*

Taking Inquiry to Scale presents my inquiry into educator collaboration and inquiry-based approaches to improving professional practice and the underlying conditions of learning and schooling. The book brings together research on inquiry approaches to professional learning in education, its implication for system-wide learning and change, and a decade of personal and shared experiences in supporting system change through system learning.

Acknowledgments

T his book is the culmination of a learning journey over several decades. Many have influenced my thinking, contributed to the resources and stories I relate here, and made this work possible.

First, I want to acknowledge my gratitude to and deep respect for the late G. Carl Ball. Nearly forty years ago, Carl and his wife, Vivian Elledge Ball, made the choice to invest their personal wealth in the greater good by endowing the Ball Foundation, which supported the work described in this book. Carl's love of learning, insatiable curiosity, and hands-on dedication to improving learning and schooling for all children serve as an exemplar of philanthropy. I also want to thank the Foundation's board of trustees for their ongoing support of the work of the Education Initiatives (EI) team, of which I have been a member for six years.

To my EI colleagues, I hope you see yourselves in this book, for it represents our learning journey and your influence on me. Thanks to you, I have actually found comfort in working in the emergent space of shared inquiry, and I am getting closer to embracing the concept that "all learning is social." To our school district partners, I thank you for inviting the EI team into your schools and into your professional lives, making it possible for us to learn with and from you. To my Human Systems Dynamics (HSD) colleagues, I thank you for helping me see the world through the lens of patterns and introducing the EI team to models and methods that greatly enriched our learning and our work. And to my NCTE colleagues, thank you for the opportunity to cocreate the online and print resources and for editorial support for this book.

I want to thank my dear friend, colleague, and mentor, Stephanie Pace Marshall, with whom my work is always better, for challenging me, supporting me, and laughing with me for nearly thirty years. I also want to thank my friend and colleague Linda Torp for months of background research and analysis and for being a critical friend as I waded through a mountain of research reports and found the gems to underpin this work.

And finally, I want to thank my family: my parents, who saw the promise of higher education and made it possible for me and for my late brother; my wife, Lynnette—best friend, partner, and support system—through all those years of graduate school, night meetings, and travel as we raised a family together; and my children, Linea and Christopher, who redefined for me what was good enough, best practice, and True North in their journeys through schooling. I love you all.

Introduction

"Inquiry," "organizational learning," and "taking change to scale" are ideas that seldom appear together in the numerous discourses of education reform. This book challenges traditional approaches to education reform by offering an alternative that embodies all three.

In the dominant narrative of education reform, changes to core education practice happen when outsiders' agendas and practices deemed universally applicable are transmitted to local educators. We see this repeatedly as school districts bring in outside experts to introduce instructional models and methods, approaches to grouping students or using time, and strategies for improving achievement for targeted students. Often these approaches are supported by evidence of their success in other settings, and educators are encouraged to apply them just as other educators have done.

A counternarrative holds that changes to core education practice happen when educators take responsibility for shared practice and student learning and build what Michael Fullan (2010) calls "collective capacity" for improving learning for all students. In this deeper narrative, educators are decision makers and change agents who build their own "reforms" that best fit students in their local settings. This book presents broad and inclusive educator inquiry as a means for building collective capacity to provide and support highly effective instruction that meets the needs of every student.

We all learn through inquiry. Each time we ask ourselves why something is or how something works, we are inquiring. As children, much of what we learned about the world around us came from asking questions, testing assumptions, and learning from our actions. Interactions with others through play, school, and daily life enriched our learning. Collaborative, inquiry-based learning designs build on this natural way of exploring and coming to understand the world.

Inquiry, as presented here, is both an approach to individual and collective learning and a habit of mind—"together a way of knowing and being in the world of education practice that . . . links individuals to larger groups . . . intended to challenge the inequities perpetuated by the educational status quo" (Cochran-Smith & Lytle, 2009, p. 120). Building collective capacity calls for collaborative professional learning designs that bring together teachers and those who support instruction to learn with and from one another. Organization-wide collaborative inquiry as described in this book engages educators in self-directed, reflective, and iterative learning from their actions that builds individual competencies and the collective capacity of schools and school districts to adapt, innovate, and respond to local needs.

The actors of education reform—educators, policymakers, researchers, and organizations supporting reform—hold different notions of "scale" and what it means to "take change to scale." For some, scale is about transmitting and replicating externally developed practices. For others, scale is about more than the reach or spread of external ideas; it's about building collaborative work and learning cultures in which educators work collaboratively to improve practice and student learning. For them, scale is measured in terms of the depth and coherence of enacting agreements and commitments to provide and support highly effective instruction.

The alternative to traditional approaches to education reform presented in this book derives from a fundamentally different theory of action. Where professional knowledge and expertise reside, the goals for change, the expectations and roles of educators and outside experts in bringing about change, and the measures of scale create a decidedly different narrative from that which most educators experience through education reform efforts.

This different theory of action challenges the thinking and practices of education reform. Policymakers are challenged to rethink the goals, approach, and measures of scale and student success. Educators are challenged to continually improve shared practice, to take ownership of their professional learning, and to share what they are learning with other educators. District and site leaders are challenged to cultivate shared agreements and commitments to instruction that meet the needs of every student, to foster agency and responsibility for shared practice and student learning, and to connect people in their shared work. Organizations supporting reform are challenged to bring together educators from all roles and levels in learning with and from one another to create conditions that support educator learning and systems change.

"Change happens from the inside out." "The knowledge and expertise needed for improvement are in the room." "*How* we do things is as important as *what* we do." For some, these are clichés. For others, they are simple truths for bringing about deep, widespread, and consequential change.

Reframing What It Means to Take Education Reform to Scale

The challenge of taking change to scale shapes how we think about change, how we work with others to bring about change, and how we determine its success. For education reform to be brought to scale—that is, to have widespread, deep, and lasting impact on schooling and student learning—change needs to permeate instruction, leadership, and the underlying organizational conditions of schools and districts.

Chapter 1 explains how an insufficient view of scale drives traditional approaches to education reform and introduces the "alternative" in terms of where solutions reside, goals for change efforts, the roles of local educators and outside experts, and measures of scale. This chapter also draws a distinction between traditional and capacity-building approaches to education reform, challenges the treatment of scale in education policy and many reform efforts, and calls out lessons learned from studies of reform efforts that yielded sustainable changes in how schools and districts provide and support instruction and student results.

Why Scale Matters

Think about a recent change introduced into your school or district. Where did it come from? How did you learn about it? What is expected of you and your colleagues? What do you think about the likelihood of its success? How we think about and act on these questions is central to bringing about change that yields meaningful and enduring results.

A Historical Perspective

For the past half-century of education reform, taking change to scale, or scaling up, typically has been seen as expanding the number of teachers or school districts implementing externally developed practices, or as the extent and ways that schools and districts respond to state and federal policy (Coburn, 2003). Beginning in the 1960s with reforms that sought to replicate models and practices deemed successful in other education settings, such as specific models for instruction or whole-school reforms, through current efforts to drive reform through legislation and education policy, the success of taking reform efforts to scale largely has been determined by their spread.

Local educators typically learn about new practices and approaches through stand-alone workshops designed primarily for outside experts to transmit information about the change, encourage "buy-in," and offer opportunities to build the understanding needed for implementing new programs, models, strategies, or policy initiatives. Thinking about bringing change to scale in this way, however, ignores the depth of learning opportunities required to build shared understanding and shared purpose for change, cultivate ownership for change, and support people in learning about, trying, and refining new practices.

Nearly forty years into the education reform era that began in the 1960s, Richard Elmore (1996) stated the problem of approaching scale as quantity or spread in this way:

> The problem of scale in educational innovation can be briefly stated as follows: innovations that require large changes in the core of educational practice seldom penetrate more than a small fraction of American schools and classrooms, and seldom last very long when they do. By the "core" of educational practice, I mean how teachers understand the nature of knowledge and the student's role in learning, how these ideas about knowledge and learning are manifested in teaching and classwork. (p. 12)

During this same period, education scholars and researchers described the challenge of taking change to scale as twofold: (1) the difficulty of changing the practice of teachers and (2) teachers working in school settings and cultures that do not support the ongoing professional learning and collaborative environments necessary to substantively change practice (Tyack & Cuban, 1995; Fullan, 1993).

An Emerging Alternative

Researchers continue to examine the complex blending of motivation, competencies, organizational conditions and culture, and infrastructure of support as a critical factor in bringing about meaningful and lasting improvement in student learning (Lena, 2011; Stoll, Bolam, McMahon, Wallace, & Thomas, 2006). An emerging body of work referred to as "capacity-building approaches" applies its findings to looking inside schools and school districts for solutions to the problems of student learning. Capacity-building approaches foster collaborative work cultures in which teachers and those in roles supporting instruction work on their practice together, thereby building "collective capacity" (Fullan, 2010) for changing education practice and improving student learning.

Through his advocacy for capacity-building approaches, Fullan (2011) calls for a shift in the goals, approach, and metrics of change. He makes the case that policymakers are using what he refers to as "the wrong drivers" for change. According to Fullan, legislation and policy directed at improving student achievement through external accountability approaches rest on the assumption that educators know more effective practices but require sanctions or rewards to enact them. Capacity-building approaches, however, assume that educators want to work more effectively but do not know how to work collectively to achieve improved results for all students. Fullan also speaks to the limitations of approaches that focus on individual educators and piecemeal or fragmented solutions that ignore the need for collective and coherent approaches to system-wide learning and change that foster intrinsic motivation in teachers and students, engage educators and students in continual improvement of instruction and learning, inspire collective or team work, and affect all teachers and students. In essence, capacity-building approaches look inside the school district for solutions centered on providing and supporting high-quality instruction that meets the needs of all students.

Capacity-building approaches to change offer an alternative to traditional approaches to education reform. While the aim of improving student achievement is the same, the source of answers to achievement problems and the goals of capacity-building approaches are quite different. Traditional reforms focus on replicating externally developed methods. Capacity-building approaches center the change effort on organizational learning in which the goal is to build the organization's capacity for adaptation and innovation to meet the challenges of unsatisfactory student achievement. Educational practices and underlying organizational conditions that have been successful in other settings are investigated and assessed in terms of those that best fit the needs of local students and the local context. Outside experts, reform models, and best practices *inform* local action; they do not *prescribe* them. In this sense, educators build their own reforms. Table 1.1 presents a comparison of traditional reform and capacity-building approaches to professional and organizational learning.

Table 1.1. Traditional and Capacity-Building Approaches to Education Reform

	Traditional Reform	**Capacity Building**
Where solutions reside	Outside the school or district	Inside the school or district
Goal for change effort	Replication of practices in expanding number of sites	Capacity to adapt, create, and respond to local needs
Role of educators and outside experts	Outside experts prescribe solutions for educators	Educators investigate problems and determine solutions together
Expectations for educators	Buy-in, follow-through, and compliance	Shared ownership and follow-through
Measures of scale	Efficacy of implementation of reform programs and policy directives	Changes in instruction, leadership, and organizational practices

Scale matters. How we think about scale raises the question of where we believe solutions reside, as well as which solutions we seek. If we believe that solutions reside outside the school district and the work of reform is to replicate externally developed programs or drive reform through state and federal policy, we naturally look to "spread" as the primary metric of scale. If we believe that solutions reside inside the school district and the work of reform is to build the system's capacity to adapt and respond to meet the needs of students, we are drawn to metrics that assess growth in the core education practice described by Elmore (1996). While both views look to spread as a measure of change, capacity-building approaches call for evidence of deeper changes in education practice and the conditions surrounding teaching and learning. How school district leaders think about what it means to take change to scale affects their goals for change, their action to foster change, and how they gauge the success of change efforts.

What It Means to Take Change to Scale

Research on scaling up education reform efforts primarily centers on the quantitative aspects of reform—that is, increasing the number of teachers, schools, or school districts involved in reform practices; costs and funding; and student achievement as measured by large-scale assessments (Fullan, 2011; Datnow, Hubbard, & Mehan, 2002). In her frequently cited analysis of the treatment of scale in the theoretical and research literature of reform implementation, Cynthia Coburn (2003) concludes:

This definition says nothing about the nature of the change envisioned or enacted or the degree to which it is sustained, or the degree to which schools and teachers have the knowledge and authority to continue to grow the reform over time. By focusing on numbers alone, traditional definitions of scale often neglect these and other qualitative measures that may be fundamental to the ability of schools to engage with a reform effort in ways that make a difference for teaching and learning. (p. 4)

Speaking to the limitations of traditional indicators of scale that mask the complex challenges of achieving what she refers to as "deep and consequential change" in education practice and conditions surrounding teaching and learning, Coburn suggests four interrelated dimensions as an alternative conceptualization of what counts as change: depth, spread, shift in ownership, and sustainability. This wider and deeper conceptualization of change alters the goals, approach, and measures of impact of improvement efforts.

Spread. Coburn's reconceptualization of scale broadens the goal of change from the spread of methods, structural reforms, and materials to include the proliferation of their underlying beliefs, norms, and principles in classrooms, schools, and districts. In Coburn's view, spread is evident in the extent and ways in which the norms and principles of the change effort become embedded in district policies, procedures, instruction, and professional learning.

Depth. While traditional reform efforts are highly focused on spread, the nature and unfolding of change receives far less attention. For Coburn, taking change to scale is a process of individual and collective learning. Depth attends to building on educators' prior knowledge by uncovering and confronting underlying assumptions about how students and adults learn, the nature of subject matter, expectations for students, and what constitutes effective instruction.

Shift in Ownership. Most reform efforts treat ownership as educator "buy-in" to new methods, procedures, and use of materials. Coburn's treatment of scale shifts the focus from encouraging educators to buy in to reforms to concentrating on the extent and ways that educators assume authority and responsibility for their individual and collective practices. Coburn contends that to take change to scale, ownership of change must shift so that it is no longer an external change controlled by external forces but rather internal change, where authority for and expertise in change reside in teachers, site leaders, and those in roles supporting instruction. She also speaks to the importance of shifting ownership to achieve spread, depth, and sustainability.

Sustainability. Coburn broadens the reform focus on sustainability from endurance of replicated practices and continued funding to a constancy of purpose that mitigates competing priorities, changing needs, shifts in politics, diminished resources, and teacher and administrative turnover. Constancy of purpose and the capacity to continually learn and adapt to current circumstances and generate solutions that best fit local needs are the primary indicators of sustainability.

Coburn's four dimensions of change call for coherent and system-wide goals, approaches, and measures of change. Taken together, the four dimensions are indicative of the change in core education practice described by Elmore (1996) and the collective capacity described by Fullan (2010) that are needed to bring about continual improvement in learning for all students. In this comprehensive and coherent view of taking change to scale, capacity building replaces replication of externally conceived reforms with organizational learning approaches that build shared purpose and expertise to foster Coburn's (2003) notion of "deep and consequential change." Capacity for adaptation and innovation replaces a push for buy-in to reforms developed far from the educators and schools for whom they are intended. Learning for students, adults, and school systems drives the goals, approaches, and measures of change.

Lessons Learned from Studies of Reform

Coburn's four dimensions of scale provide a lens for examining the extent to which and ways that change manifests in schools and districts. Researchers have applied these dimensions when analyzing reform interventions applied across schools and districts, as well as for in-depth analysis of change within individual schools and districts. Both views yield lessons for changing core education practice and taking change to scale.

Large-Scale Reform Efforts in the United States and Abroad

As a major funder of education reform, the Ford Foundation engaged the RAND Corporation to examine the scale-up process of fifteen large-scale education reform efforts in the United States and abroad (Glennan, Bodilly, Galegher, & Kerr, 2004). The reforms included models, programs, designs, and interventions focused on improving existing practices of teaching and learning in classrooms. All the reform efforts were implemented in multiple school districts, and their scope ranged from sixty to more than one thousand schools each. While most efforts centered on individual schools, some focused on whole-district improvement. Each of the reform efforts previously had documented changes in teaching practices and improvements in student performance and achievement. From their analysis of the scale-up experiences, and using Coburn's four dimensions of scale, the RAND researchers identified two key factors in taking reform approaches to scale:

1. *Broad, inclusive, and iterative learning experiences,* noting that "the scale-up process is necessarily iterative and complex and requires the support of multiple actors" (p. 647), and "scaling up will continue to require an iterative process of learning by doing" (p. 652)

2. *Broad, inclusive, and coherent infrastructure* to support educator learning and system change, stating that "[i]f scale-up is to succeed, the actors involved . . . must jointly address a set of known, interconnected tasks, especially aligning policies and infrastructure in coherent ways to sustain practice" (pp. 647–48); "schools and districts must . . . provide a supportive and coherent infrastructure if new practices are to take root and grow" (651); and "a coherent set of practices for teaching, learning, and assessment" (p. 652)

An In-depth Look at One School District's Change Effort

A study of reform in a single school district provides deeper insight into the nature of organizational learning experiences required for scaling. Researchers Janet Chrispeels and Margarita Gonzalez (2006) analyzed an education reform effort involving a partnership between a university and a school district, also using Coburn's four dimensions of scale to understand the partnership's impact on the school district. At the time of the partnership, the rapidly growing central California coast school district served approximately 16,000 students in sixteen elementary and three middle schools.

Through their three-year partnership, the university and the district staff collaborated to bring about changes in four key areas of district-wide practice: aligning the curriculum; setting an instructional focus to improve reading comprehension and writing and meeting the needs of English learners; developing a leadership academy for all administrators; and increasing the accessibility and use of data, especially district and state assessment results, to determine areas for improvement.

While these are common focus areas for school and district reform, what stands out in this example is the comprehensiveness of the reform effort and the approaches taken by the partnership to effect change. In short, the partnership did the "right things" according to traditional reform approaches. As a result of the partnership, the district's curriculum became more coherent and aligned with instruction and assessment, achievement improved overall and for targeted students, administrators reported high satisfaction with their professional learning experiences, and the accessibility and use of data increased. Support for maintaining many of the system-wide changes, however, was short-lived. A long history of tensions between the teachers' union and central administration culminated in the union successfully electing its two new candidates to the board of education, the assistant superintendent for educational services resigning, and the superintendent announcing his retirement.

Sharing their lessons learned, Chrispeels and Gonzalez (2006) stress the centrality of ownership as a necessary foundation for deep and lasting change, quoting Coburn (2003): "[T]o be considered 'at scale,' ownership over the reform must shift so that it is no longer an 'external' reform, controlled by a reformer, but rather becomes an 'internal' reform with authority for the reform held by districts, schools, and teachers who have the capacity to sustain, spread, and deepen reform principles themselves" (p. 6).

For change to endure, it must be cocreated and co-owned by stakeholders. It is not enough to inform stakeholders of the need for change, give a sound rationale for selected approaches, and provide training. Those with responsibility for implementing change and accountability for its results, and those affected by the change, need to own it. Whether tacit or explicit, present or lacking, agreements and assumptions about learning, teaching, priorities, goals, and approaches to improvement impact the likelihood of deep and lasting change.

Chrispeels and Gonzalez (2006) also speak to the importance of reform approaches building on existing strengths. They explain that most reform approaches are deficit focused and center on problems targeting achievement deficits and gaps, as well as practices or conditions deemed ineffective or unsatisfactory. Seldom do reform approaches look for, acknowledge, or build on existing strengths present in a school or district, thereby bypassing opportunities to affirm good work and achievements, engender motivation for the difficult work of change ahead, and build a connection between the past and the future.

Conclusion

Studies of reform interventions illustrate the importance of educator collaborative practice—collaborative work and collaborative professional learning embedded in actual work—for bringing education reform to scale. Findings from these studies yield three lessons for educators, policymakers, and organizations supporting education reform. Scalable reforms, those that result in deep, meaningful, and lasting change to core education practice and student results, entail:

1. Professional learning that is collaborative, situated in actual work, and grounded in iterative cycles of practice and reflection;

2. Broad and inclusive learning experiences during which educators from multiple sites, roles, and levels work with shared purpose and learn with and from one another; and,

3. Broad and inclusive infrastructure to support collaborative work and collaborative professional learning embedded in actual work.

Building on these lessons learned, the remaining chapters examine the extent to which and ways that a collaborative inquiry approach to capacity building offers a viable and scalable alternative to traditional approaches to education reform.

2

There Is Something Powerful about Inquiry

Collaborative inquiry situates professional learning in iterative cycles of practice and shared reflection. Studies of collaborative inquiry approaches to professional learning reveal effective changes in instruction, leadership practices, and student results. While collaborative inquiry and other job-embedded approaches to professional learning are not new, education reform in the United States more typically stresses replicating methods and structures over the deep and rigorous investigations of shared practice that characterize collaborative inquiry. Capturing the potential of collaborative inquiry as a scalable alternative to traditional approaches to education reform requires understanding and a willingness to apply the aspects of inquiry that contribute to student results.

Chapter 2 provides a historical overview of inquiry approaches to professional learning and the findings of studies that investigate and link collaborative educator inquiry to student results. Based on this review of the literature, the chapter identifies and describes six key elements of collaborative inquiry approaches that yield student results.

Inquiry and Educator Professional Learning

Student learning will improve when educators take ownership of their professional learning. This is not a new idea. Nearly a century ago, John Dewey envisioned teachers engaged in rigorous investigations of their practice in a process he called "reflective thinking" (1933). The process he outlined—formulating a problem, reasoning from evidence, developing hypotheses, testing hypotheses, and then reformulating based on feedback from experience—forms the basis of current inquiry approaches to professional learning.

Looking Back over the Past Half-Century

Educator professional learning in the United States shifted direction markedly in the late 1960s. Policymakers concerned about our nation's educational competitiveness and the need to increase the numbers of graduates in the fields of mathematics and science following the Russian launch of *Sputnik* in 1957 passed the Elementary and Secondary Education Act (1965), making funding available for teacher professional development. School districts typically used these funds to provide one-size-fits-all and short-term professional development programs. These programs often treated teachers as "passive and sometimes resistant learners with deficiencies in knowledge or skills that could be addressed through prepackaged workshops and inservice sessions" (Thibodeau, 2008 p. 55).

The 1980s and 1990s saw a rekindling of Dewey's call for reflective thinking as the basis for teachers' professional learning. During this time, school districts increasingly supported groups of teachers in learning to use inquiry methods in the form of action research to investigate instructional topics of interest to them. Action research—engaging as a researcher and directly learning from the experience of conducting the research in one's work setting—emerged as an alternative to district-led workshops designed with little or no involvement from teachers (Bray, 2002). While teachers often shared the results of their action research with one another, action research projects were typically individual inquiries into instructional practice.

During this period, professional development in the form of teachers working in collaborative groups in elementary school settings became an important factor in school improvement efforts (DuFour, 2004; Duke, 2004). While these activities were not necessarily the rigorous investigations of practice envisioned by Dewey, teachers and school leaders actively engaged in investigating and resolving issues of importance to them. Researchers have identified links between these collaborative, school-based professional learning approaches and positive changes in teacher practices (Little, 2003), teacher willingness to use innovative materials and methods (Talbert & McLaughlin, 2002), and improved student achievement (Gallimore, Ermeling, Saunders, & Goldenberg, 2009; Timperley & Parr, 2007; Vescio, Ross, & Adams, 2006; Thompson, Gregg, & Niska, 2004). Similar collaborative professional development approaches were not characteristic of secondary schools during this time.

The passage of the No Child Left Behind Act (2001) and ensuing reforms greatly altered the support for and direction of professional learning provided by schools and school districts. Time and other support for teacher-directed inquiry was sacrificed for professional learning that responded to the urgency of meeting mandates designed to improve overall achievement and close achievement gaps. While continuing on a more limited basis and supported by professional learning standards (Learning Forward, 2011) and professional education associations, teacher-directed professional learning competes with predominantly district- and school-directed one-size-fits-all approaches, with limited teacher involvement in design and delivery (Gallimore et al., 2009). The pendulum has swung back to professional learning modes of the late 1960s and 1970s.

Collaborative Inquiry Approaches to Educator Professional Learning

Studies in the United States and Abroad

The research and evaluation studies of collaborative inquiry-based approaches to educator professional learning cited in this book represent individual research studies, analyses of multiple research studies, and evaluation reports of long-term projects conducted in the United States and abroad. These studies represent nearly 400 schools in urban, rural, and suburban settings. While the majority of studies focus on elementary schools, 25 percent involve middle and high school educators. One study looks at a community college. Ninety-one studies, approximately 25 percent, took place in New Zealand, where collaborative inquiry is a common approach to educator professional learning.

The research studies describe how educators engage in collaborative inquiry and its impact on their practice, the underlying organizational conditions in their schools, and student results. While most studies use large-scale assessments, such as state assessments, as measures of student achievement, nearly a dozen studies include other measures of student results. The evaluation studies describe multiyear projects in which educators engaged in collaborative inquiry and identify the impact of collaborative inquiries on educator practice and the organizational conditions in their schools. These studies also report on the impact of collaborative inquiry approaches to organizational learning and problem solving.

Researchers use different language, sometimes interchangeably, to identify groups of educators engaged in collaborative inquiry: *inquiry groups, communities of practice, professional learning communities,* and *inquiry teams* are among the most frequent terms. All engage educators in answering a question or resolving a problem of importance to them relating to student learning; all involve educators learning with and from one another; and all cultivate educator ownership of their practice.

Researchers approach collaborative inquiry by examining its *attributes*, such as describing the nature of collaboration and self-direction or the nature of learning from continuous cycles of planning, action, and reflection (Ball Foundation, 2011; Bruce, 2009; Thibodeau, 2008; Timperley & Parr, 2007; Vescio et al., 2006; Zech, Gause-Vega, Bray, Secules, & Goldman, 2000). A much smaller number of studies approach collaborative inquiry as a *process* involving a protocol of specified actions or conditions (Gallimore et al., 2009; Parsons, 2009).

The majority of studies of collaborative inquiry-based professional learning in education center on school-based approaches. Most studies involve groups of teachers such as grade-level or department teams. Another cluster of studies involves whole-school involvement. A much smaller group of studies involves groups of teachers from multiple schools, including those participating in online professional learning experiences.

With the exception of the two evaluation studies (Ball, 2011; Parsons, 2009), the literature lacks district-wide studies or organizational applications of inquiry in the United States in which teachers and other educators jointly learn, plan, and solve problems across school districts. The potential for collaborative inquiry to act as a catalyst for personal and organizational or district-wide learning and change remains untested in the research literature (Brooks & Watkins, 1994).

The role of experts in collaborative inquiry approaches to educator professional learning also varies in the literature. While ownership of professional learning distinguishes collaborative inquiry from other professional learning approaches, experts frequently play a role in educator inquiries. In some studies, inquiries are guided by facilitators with content area and pedagogical expertise (Thibodeau, 2008; Zech et al., 2000). In other studies, inquiries are guided by facilitators with expertise in guiding inquiry and collaborative learning (Ball Foundation, 2011; Thibodeau, 2008; Timperley & Parr, 2007; Zech et al., 2000). Other studies involve inquiries guided by trained peer facilitators (Gallimore et al., 2009; Zech et al., 2000). In all instances of facilitated inquiries, the role of facilitators became more that of a co-inquirer as inquiry progressed.

What Happens When Educators Engage in Collaborative Inquiry

Studies of collaborative inquiry-based professional learning in K–12 education primarily focus on the application of inquiry methods by teachers to investigate problems and questions relating to teaching and student learning. Some of the studies include site leaders (principals, teacher-leaders, and others such as instructional coaches). What follows is an overview of research findings related to the impact of collaborative inquiry-based approaches on instructional and leadership practice, student results, and the organizational conditions in schools where teachers and site leaders engage in collaborative inquiry.

Instructional Practice

The findings on the impact of collaborative inquiry-based professional learning on teacher instructional practice fall into two broad areas: impact related directly to instructional practice and impact related to dispositions regarding professional learning and its relationship to practice.

Studies reveal changes in the instructional practice of teachers at all levels of schooling:

Elementary level	Teachers at the elementary level participating in school-based professional learning communities demonstrated sustained changes in literacy instructional strategies and used a wider range of indicators of student learning. (Timperley & Parr, 2007)
	Teachers at the elementary level participating in school-based professional learning communities demonstrated more student-centered and differentiated instructional strategies. (Vescio et al., 2006)
	Teachers at the elementary and secondary levels participating in collaborative inquiry groups demonstrated increased coherence in literacy instructional practices. (Timperley & Parr, 2007)
Secondary level	Teachers at the secondary level participating in collaborative and guided inquiries into literacy practices demonstrated sustained changes in student-centered instructional practices. (Thibodeau, 2008)
	Teachers at the secondary level participating in collaborative inquiry study groups shifted their instructional practice from having students memorize facts to promoting students' deeper understanding of content in mathematics, science, and social science. (Zech et al., 2000)

| Community college level | Community college faculty participating in collaborative inquiry groups incorporated a broader range of evidence-based decision making regarding student learning. (Parsons, 2009) |
| | Community college faculty participating in collaborative inquiry groups diversified their teaching strategies. (Parsons, 2009) |

Studies reveal changes in teacher thinking about their professional learning and its relationship to their practice:

Focus and persistence	Elementary school teachers participating in inquiry teams maintained shared and persistent focus on problems of practice when using a collaborative inquiry protocol. (Gallimore et al., 2009)
	Site-based teacher inquiry teams at the elementary level sustained inquiry into problems of practice focused on student achievement at elementary and secondary levels. (Gallimore et al., 2009)
	Teachers at the elementary and secondary levels participating in communities of practice conducted yearlong self-directed inquiries into questions of instructional practice. (Ball Foundation, 2011)
Ownership and accountability	Elementary and secondary teachers participating in communities of practice reported growing regard for their work as practice; they also demonstrated greater attentiveness to preparation and reflection and deepened accountability for their practice. (Ball Foundation, 2011)
	Teachers participating in online communities of practice (Bruce, 2009) and teachers participating in professional learning communities (Zech et al., 2000) demonstrated ownership of their practice in the form of self-initiated, self-monitored, and self-regulated learning.
Self-efficacy	Teachers in elementary schools participating in inquiry teams shifted attribution of improved student performance to their teaching rather than to external causes. (Gallimore et al., 2009)

Receptivity to new ideas	Community college faculty participating in collaborative inquiry groups were more receptive to new and diverse ideas relating to instruction. (Parsons, 2009)

Leadership Practice

Studies revealed three effects of the engagement of site leaders in collaborative inquiry-based professional learning.

Greater coherence in leadership practices	Elementary and secondary site leaders participating in school-based professional learning communities demonstrated increased coherence in leadership practices. (Timperley & Parr, 2007)
Use of data and evidence-based practices	Elementary and secondary site leaders participating in collaborative inquiry demonstrated increased use of data and other evidence in planning for instruction and school improvement practices. (Ball Foundation, 2011; Timperley & Parr, 2007)
Site leaders perceived as instructional leaders	In elementary and secondary schools where site leaders participated in collaborative inquiry, faculty increasingly perceived site leadership teams as instructional leaders. (Ball Foundation, 2011)

Underlying Organizational Conditions

The findings on the impact of educators' engagement in collaborative inquiry professional learning reveal a multitude of effects on organizational conditions in their schools:

Content and format of faculty meetings	In schools where teachers and site leadership teams participated in collaborative inquiries, site meetings were increasingly collaborative, driven by what teachers wanted to learn, and characterized by inquiry practices and use of student data for planning and decision making. (Ball Foundation, 2011)
Collaborative professional learning	In schools where teachers and site leadership teams participated in collaborative inquiries, professional learning was increasingly collaborative. (Ball Foundation, 2011)

Organizational involvement	Community college faculty who participated in collaborative inquiry groups were involved more frequently in college leadership activities. (Parsons, 2009)
Connections vs. isolation	In school districts where teachers and site leadership teams participated in collaborative inquiry, the experience fostered the creation of networks of teachers, thereby breaking isolation and shifting the working cultures of schools. (Ball Foundation, 2011; Bray, 2002)
	Community college faculty who participated in collaborative inquiry groups demonstrated more frequent linkages with faculty in other colleges using the same collaborative inquiry protocols. (Parsons, 2009)
Shared meaning and focus	In a midsize urban school district where elementary and secondary teachers and site leadership teams engaged in collaborative inquiries, evaluators found evidence of an increased connection of participants' work to district priorities, a more shared and coherent vision of effective instruction, common school improvement priorities, common language, and shared focus of site leadership teams. (Ball Foundation, 2011)
	In schools where teachers participated in collaborative inquiry, there was evidence of increased collaboration and shared understandings and commitments regarding instruction. (King, 2002)
Coherence in instruction and leadership practice	In schools where teachers participated in professional learning communities, there was increased coherence in instructional and leadership practices at all levels of the school district. (Timperley & Parr, 2007)
	In a midsize urban school district where teachers and site leadership teams engaged in collaborative inquiries, there was a proliferation of collaboration and inquiry-based practices in site and district meetings. (Ball Foundation, 2011)

Student Results

The findings on the impact of collaborative inquiry-based professional learning on students fall into three broad areas: overall student achievement, achievement for targeted groups of students, and students' understanding of content knowledge.

Improved
achievement
overall

Elementary Schools

In elementary schools serving high numbers of low-achieving students with limited English proficiency and where grade-level teams of teachers participated in teacher inquiry teams, student achievement as measured by the Stanford 9 test increased significantly in comparison with similar schools where teachers did not participate in teacher inquiry teams. (McDougall, Saunders, & Goldenberg, 2007)

In rural elementary schools where teachers participated in professional learning communities to develop instructional strategies based on student data, students performing at or above grade level increased from 50 percent to 80 percent. (Berry, Johnson, & Montgomery, 2005)

Middle Schools

In middle schools where teachers participated in professional learning communities focused on individual student achievement data, student achievement results on state tests in reading, writing, math, science, and social studies increased dramatically. (Phillips, 2003)

In middle schools where teachers participated in professional learning communities in which conversations were characterized by data-driven dialogue, the percentage of students meeting or exceeding state learning standards increased from 50 percent to 75 percent. (Strahan, 2003)

Secondary Schools

In secondary schools where teachers participated in collaborative inquiries of literacy instruction, students demonstrated self-directed learning and increased achievement. (Thibodeau, 2008)

K–12 Schools

In two large urban school districts where K–12 teachers engaged in structured, sustained, and supported instructional conversations, and where teachers investigated the relationships between instructional practices and student work, significant gains in student learning were identified. (Supovitz & Christman, 2003; Supovitz, 2002)

Improved achievement for targeted students	In elementary schools where teachers participated in collaborative inquiries into literacy instructional practices, students scoring at the lower 20 percent of achievement tests significantly improved their test results. (Timperley & Parr, 2007)
	In schools where second- and third-grade teachers collaborated on data-driven inquiries focused on improving literacy achievement, students increased achievement on state achievement tests at significantly higher rates than comparable students in the school district. (Hollins, McIntyre, DeBose, Hollins, & Towner, 2004)
Deeper understanding of content knowledge	In secondary schools where teachers participated in inquiries focused on instructional practices relating to students' acquisition of content knowledge, students demonstrated deeper understanding of content knowledge in mathematics, science, and social science. (Zech et al., 2000)

These findings indicate shifts in educator thinking and actions. Instruction, actions, and conditions that support instruction, as well as student results, improved when educators engaged in collaborative inquiries centered on resolving issues of student learning.

Key Elements of Collaborative Educator Inquiry

Linking Inquiry Approaches and Student Results

Research and evaluation studies strongly support the linkage between educator engagement in collaborative inquiry approaches to professional learning and improved professional practice, student results, and underlying organizational conditions that support student learning. Collaborative educator inquiries can take place in a variety of settings, with or without inquiry protocols, and with different types of support. So what makes for a successful collaborative inquiry learning experience?

Studies of collaborative educator inquiry are rich with examples of educators learning together from their practice. While the studies vary in scope, setting, and process, clusters, or patterns of related actions that make up key elements of collaborative inquiry, are apparent. Taken together, these key elements distinguish collaborative inquiry from other collaborative approaches to educator professional learning in which educators learn about new methods outside of the context of their practice. Such approaches are *about* practice but do not engage educators in learning *from* practice.

Six key elements of collaborative inquiry lead to improved educator practice, improved student results, and improved organizational conditions that support student learning:

- Investigate shared problems or questions of practice.
- Learn with and from colleagues.
- Seek expertise and perspectives of others beyond the inquiry group.
- Use evidence and data.
- Act, reflect, and refine practice.
- Share and connect learning.

Investigate shared problems or questions of practice. Inquiries that lead to more effective professional practice and improved student results were self-directed and centered on investigating issues of student learning. Inquiries began with coming to a shared understanding of the student achievement problem and how current practices and organizational conditions affect achievement. Inquiries centered on *how, why,* and *under what conditions* practices and organizational conditions produce results. The participants guided the inquiries, in some instances with and in other instances without external facilitators. They came together as whole faculties, grade-level teams, or subject area teams and sometimes crossed school sites. Participants investigated their practice and were active participants in constructing meaning and knowledge. In most studies, participation was voluntary; in other studies, participation was a condition of being a member of the faculty. In all cases, participants acted as researchers, not as research subjects or recipients of methods or strategies prescribed by others.

Examples of issues of professional practice and questions related to student learning included:

Elementary school	Helping students understand multiplication as repeated addition (Gallimore et al., 2009)
	Student academic problems related to low literacy achievement (Timperley & Parr, 2007)
	Engaging parents in meaningful and sustainable relationships that support student literacy (Ball Foundation, 2011)
Middle school	Second language learners' use of proper punctuation and capitalization (Gallimore et al., 2009)

	Students' understanding of concepts and principles beyond the accumulation of facts and procedures in content areas (Zech et al., 2000)
	Raising the fluency and literacy levels for second language learners (Ball Foundation, 2011)
High school	Students' analysis of data and reporting results in conclusion sections of laboratory reports (Gallimore et al., 2009)
	Content area teaching strategies that help students become more active, independent, and successful readers of content area texts (Timperley & Parr, 2007)
	Differentiation of instruction in heterogeneous secondary classrooms (Ball Foundation, 2011)
Community college	Do peer study groups enhance student learning? How well do students who take developmental education courses when they enter college perform in subsequent courses?
	What connections within the college do adjunct faculty need to be successful in their teaching? (Parsons, 2009)

Learn with and from colleagues. Collaboration provided a supportive context for inquiries into teaching and leadership practices and their impact on student learning. Collaborative inquiries were shared and participatory learning experiences in which participants contributed to the design and conduct of the inquiries and reflected on experience obtained through taking action on the inquiries. Being equal partners, all participants had the power to shape and act on the question or issue being investigated and to contribute to shared meaning acquired from the inquiry experience. Dialogue, or conversation between colleagues, was at the core of interrogating practice, constructing meaning, and sharing new knowledge.

Seek expertise and perspectives of others beyond the inquiry group. Inquiries that yielded improved student results looked outside of the collective knowledge and expertise of participants to inform the inquiries. Some studies included others outside the inquiry group who possessed content and pedagogical expertise related to the inquiry focus. Some studies included the perspectives of those outside of education such as families and community members. Other studies involved facilitators trained in the inquiry process to help participants maintain focus on collaboration and inquiry. All of the studies sought grounded, or evidence-based, knowledge drawing from expertise such as research, theory, best practices, and diverse perspectives related to the inquiry focus.

Use evidence and data. Evidence and data played a central role in all inquiries. Many studies made reference to No Child Left Behind (NCLB) and its requirement that disaggregated achievement data be used to examine achievement for targeted subgroups of students. Data about students, their achievement, and the broader school and community context enabled inquiry participants to analyze and investigate the student achievement problems at the center of the inquiries. Classroom and meeting observations, instructional artifacts, and interviews provided data and evidence relating to educator practice. Student results were determined by collecting and examining achievement data, usually from state-wide assessments, and data from formative, classroom-based assessments and student work samples. Other forms of evidence such as curriculum artifacts and recordings of observations provided a broader way for participants to understand the impact of their actions on student results. Evidence and data were the basis for understanding and sharing what happened as participants acted on new learning acquired through their inquiries.

Act, reflect, and refine practice. Recurring cycles of planning, action, and reflection on the results of one's action are the heart of inquiry—individual and collaborative. The studies do not portray inquiry as a process of discrete or linear steps; instead, researchers characterize inquiry as being *iterative* and *recursive*. They describe the iterative aspect of collaborative inquiry as involving repeated cycles of planning, acting, and reflecting that build on previous cycles and inform subsequent cycles. The recursive aspect of collaborative inquiry involves the continuous reexamination of the inquiry question or problem based on what emerges from seeking the expertise and experience of others, using data and other evidence, and engaging colleagues in learning from actions taken in testing new learning in practice.

All of the studies point to the reflective aspect of collaborative inquiry as an essential element of inquiry learning and something that distinguishes collaborative inquiry from other approaches to professional learning. Repeated cycles of planning, action, and reflection engage participants in understanding why actions, or new methods, lead to certain results. Professional learning becomes more than the accumulation of methods; it becomes an investigation of individual and collective practice. Participants gain a deeper understanding of how and why actions make a difference for students. Researchers also cite evidence that collaboration provides a supportive context for sustained reflection on teaching practices and student learning.

Share and connect learning. Study participants shared what they learned through their inquiries in several ways. They talked about their inquiries at faculty meetings and other school convenings. In some instances, they participated in inquiries with colleagues from other schools. When collaborative inquiries included significant numbers of teachers within a school or school district, researchers found more coherent instructional practice and organizational conditions. Successful inquiries built shared understanding and individual and collective competencies among participants.

While sharing and connecting learning was the weakest of the patterns of related actions, this key element holds the potential to connect individual, group, and organizational district-wide learning. The remainder of this book is dedicated to supporting the sharing and connecting of professional learning through collaborative inquiries at all levels and scales in a school district.

Table 2.1 lists the key elements of collaborative inquiry and their related actions identified through a review of research and evaluation studies of collaborative inquiry approaches to educator professional learning.

Conclusion: Distinguishing Collaborative Inquiry from Other Approaches to Educator Professional Learning

Collaborative inquiry offers an alternative to one-size-fits-all and top-down approaches to educator professional learning through its approach and its results. Collaborative inquiry changes the professional learning experience by reframing how professional knowledge is constructed and applied. Moving from professional learning approached as the acquisition of methods and structures developed outside the classroom and the school, collaborative inquiry places educators in the role of actively constructing professional knowledge through treating their classrooms and schools as sites for investigation.

Professional learning centers on investigating shared problems or questions of practice as they relate to student learning. The student learning problem, not a prepackaged one-size-fits-all solution, is the departure point for inquiry. Recurring cycles of planning, action, and reflection characterize the professional learning experience. Educators engage in learning and conversation from inside their practice and build on their professional knowledge by examining and reflecting on new learning through the lens of prior knowledge and experience, new information and data, and the impact of their actions.

Collaborative inquiry engages educators in self-directed and participatory learning, moving beyond collective passive learning to learning with and from colleagues through action and reflection. In the supportive context of collaborative inquiry, participants explore agreements and disagreements about learn-

Table 2.1. Research-Based Key Elements of Collaborative Inquiry

Key Elements	Related Actions
Investigate shared problems or questions of practice.	Participants share and largely self-direct voluntary investigations of professional practice as they relate to issues of student learning. Participants construct knowledge of practice from reflection on their actions and the actions of others. Participants are not research subjects or passive recipients of knowledge created by others.
Learn with and from colleagues.	The inquiry is a shared, supportive, and participatory learning experience. New meaning/knowledge/understanding is constructed through conversation with co-inquirers. Participants are responsible for their own learning.
Seek expertise and perspectives of others beyond the inquiry group.	Inquiry seeks grounded knowledge from research, theory, and best practices. Inquiry seeks expert knowledge and experience; inquiry seeks the perspectives of those who may see the student learning problem differently. Each participant serves as a resource for sharing, finding, and constructing new knowledge; some participants have more knowledge about the subject than others, yet all have experience to contribute.
Use evidence and data.	Evidence and data are means for framing/understanding/exploring the student learning problem and sharing with others in the inquiry and beyond. Inquiry includes quantitative and qualitative indicators related to the learning issue. Data involve students, their performance, and family/school/community contexts as related to the student learning issue. Inquiry seeks grounded knowledge.
Act, reflect, and refine practice.	Recurring cycles of plan–act–reflect build on previous cycles and inform subsequent cycles. Participants learn for and about practice from experience/action and reflection.
Share and connect learning.	Learning is shared among inquiry participants, within schools, and district-wide.

ing and teaching, uncover tacit knowledge, and come to individual and shared understandings of how, why, and under what conditions instruction and leadership yield positive student results.

The results of educator engagement in collaborative inquiry speak to its effectiveness and viability as an approach to educator professional learning. Evidence of improved instructional practice, increased student achievement, and organizational conditions that support high achievement are documented in multiple studies involving elementary and secondary schools in various settings serving diverse student populations. Results also demonstrate increased teacher agency in their practice and ownership of their professional learning. The persistent problem of transferring new learning into practice is overcome by centering professional learning on practice. Through collaborative inquiry, individual and collective action become more intentional, coherent, and evidence based.

3

Tapping the Potential of Collaborative Inquiry for System-Wide Learning

While studies of collaborative inquiry approaches to professional learning reveal changes in educator practice and student results, nearly all of these applications involve groups of educators working and learning in isolation from one another. The potential for realizing district-wide or organizational learning and change remains untapped from such siloed efforts. Broad and inclusive applications of collaborative inquiry that gather together educators from all roles, levels, and sites can bridge this gap and bring the results attainable by small groups to a district-wide scale.

Chapter 3 examines the similarities and differences between group and system-wide approaches to collaborative inquiry and describes a broad, inclusive application of collaborative inquiry in a midsize urban school district. This chapter introduces and describes a set of design principles that enable the scaling of collaborative inquiry as a capacity-building approach to district-wide learning and change.

Inquiry and System-Wide Learning

Similarities and Differences between Group and System-Wide Approaches

System-wide approaches to collaborative inquiry greatly expand its scope and potential impact. Table 3.1 illustrates how system-wide collaborative inquiry approaches involve more than increasing the number of individuals and groups engaged in inquiry. Participation includes educators in various roles that support instruction, and the focus of the inquiries expands to a broader array of practices and underlying conditions that affect teaching and learning.

Table 3.1. Similarities and Differences between Group and System-Wide Approaches to Collaborative Inquiry

	Group Approaches	System-Wide Approaches
Participants	Teams and groups of educators, primarily teachers	Multiple and connected teams and groups of teachers and other educators in roles that support instruction, such as principals, instructional coaches, district and executive administrators
Focus	Investigating instructional issues as they relate to student learning	Investigating issues of instruction, leadership, and underlying organizational conditions within schools and district-wide as they relate to student learning
Impact	Instruction in participants' classrooms Leadership and underlying organizational conditions in participants' schools Achievement of students whose teachers participate in collaborative inquiries	Shared agreements around instruction More coherent instruction, leadership, and underlying organizational conditions district-wide Student achievement district-wide

Implications for a System-Wide Approach

While the research findings for group approaches to collaborative inquiry reveal key elements of the nature of collaborative inquiry, these findings do not provide sufficient insight and direction for taking collaborative inquiry to scale as a system-wide capacity-building approach. A different frame of reference is needed to accommodate the broader participation, expanded focus, and scope of potential impact. The field of organizational learning provides a frame of reference for understanding how organizations learn, adapt, and thrive in fulfilling their purpose and achieving results that are important to them.

The term *organizational learning* refers to the ability of members of an organization to gain insight and understanding from their experiences through experimentation, observation, analysis, and a willingness to examine successes and failures (McGill, Slocum, & Goldenberg, 1992). This view of collective (organizational) learning is markedly similar to inquiry learning framed by the key elements of collaborative inquiry described in Chapter 1. Both views describe participatory and reflective learning processes grounded in shared work experiences. While there are differences between school districts and other organizational contexts, the goal of becoming more fit and more effective at achieving their purpose in the face of challenging and changing circumstances is the same.

The underlying premise of organizational learning is that people can marry their individual aspirations to better organizational performance (Serrat, 2009). This is fundamental to achieving shared purpose. In his widely studied and referenced *The Fifth Discipline,* Peter Senge (1990) describes learning organizations of various types. For Senge a learning organization is one that through its people continues to learn and adapt to achieve its desired results. An organization changes and becomes more effective through its people learning with and from one another in their work contexts. Senge goes on to explain that the capacity for change resides in building and strengthening the connections of people and their shared work. Figure 3.1 depicts this dynamic.

Figure 3.1. Building Capacity for Systems Learning and Change

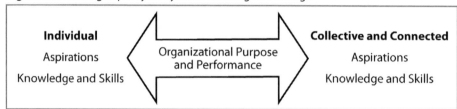

Organizational learning is a useful frame of reference for thinking about taking collaborative inquiry to scale as an approach to systems learning and capacity building. In an organizational learning context, collaborative inquiry occurs in ways that engage educators in various roles across a school district in investigating shared questions and problems of learning and teaching. Because educators learn with and from one another, actions to improve teaching and learning are more likely to become connected within a school and across a school district. Collaborative inquiry pursued in this way leads to more focused and coherent practices and organizational conditions that make increased student achievement more likely. New knowledge is generated from and tested in practice and then refined with the support of colleagues across the school and the district. Through an organizational learning approach to collaborative inquiry, individuals learn and the organization learns, thereby building the competencies of people and the capacity of schools and school districts for highly effective instruction.

Designing for Scale

Beginning in 1999, the Education Initiatives (EI) team of the Ball Foundation partnered with five midsize urban school districts across the country for the purpose of building the districts' capacity to provide and support highly effective literacy instruction and improving literacy achievement for all students. Over time these partnerships were increasingly framed as collaborative inquiries into instructional and leadership practice and the underlying organizational conditions of those schools and districts.

Through these school district partnerships, the Foundation identified and refined a set of seven design principles that support collaborative inquiry taken to the scale of system-wide learning. The Ball Foundation's design principles for organizational learning and capacity building are listed in Figure 3.2 (Ball Foundation, 2010b).

A helpful way to think about a system-wide approach to collaborative inquiry is as a particular application of the key elements of collaborative inquiry (see Table 2.1, p. 24). In this particular *system-wide* application guided by the design principles, the key elements contribute to focused and coherent actions and conditions that support both student learning and professional learning.

The design principles are not unique. What is unique is naming and defining the principles, as the Ball Foundation did, and then applying them as an approach to district-wide professional learning. When applied in the presence of the relationships and patterns of connectedness they foster, the design principles contributed to fundamental changes in instructional and leadership practice and organizational conditions in partner school districts (Babiera & Preskill, 2010; Ball Foundation, 2010b).

Figure 3.2. Design Principles for Organizational Learning and Capacity Building

Build shared purpose	Bring people together to discover what they really care about, determine their highest aspirations for students and themselves, and invite them into something larger than themselves.
Access the capacity of stakeholders	Engage staff, students, parents, and community members in learning about the school district, sharing what is important, and making choices about what is best for schools and the district.
Work in systemic ways	Engage people in ways that help them achieve what is important to the school district by gaining access to one another and to information and by seeing interconnections between grade levels, subject areas, schools, families, neighborhoods, processes, and relationships.
Use inquiry to guide practice	Bring people together in dialogue, learning, and reflection so that they ask questions that matter, make their practice visible to others, seek relevant information and data, and plan and implement actions with ongoing reflection and feedback.
Attend to content and process	Create learning processes and experiences that engage people in making meaning and finding connections between information, people, and situations.
Create adaptive solutions	Cocreate with partners ways to acquire, share, and use information that generate new relationships and connections to solve problems.
Build on assets	Identify and build on strengths, values, traditions, practices, and accomplishments.

The design principles are grounded in theory, research, and practice in the fields of human and adult learning, organizational development, systems and complexity, and the Ball Foundation's partnership experiences. The design principles enact shared beliefs that are basic assumptions the Foundation accepts as true. Through its partnerships, the Foundation also has identified underlying conditions that support organizational learning and capacity building. The expanded explication of the design principles can be found in Appendix A, as well as online at www.literacyinlearningexchange.org/design-principles-organizational-learning-change.

A Tale of Three Inquiries: Examples of a System-Wide Approach to Collaborative Inquiry

This portion of the chapter relates the story of the Ball Foundation's five-year partnership with a midsize urban school district in Southern California through three iterative examples of system-wide collaborative inquiry framed by the document "Design Principles for Organizational Learning and Capacity Building" (Babiera, 2008). The inquiries took place at the beginning, middle, and conclusion of the partnership.

The six-member Education Initiatives team of the Ball Foundation partnered with a school district of twenty-three elementary and secondary schools and 23,000 students to cocreate organizational learning experiences that engaged educators from all levels, kindergarten through grade 12, who provided and supported instruction, including teachers, district program leaders, and site, district, and executive leaders. Together, the EI team and school district educators designed the inquiries and created collaborative learning structures such as school leadership teams and communities of practice that engaged district educators in purposeful, participatory, and reflective learning and problem solving to improve the quality of instruction for their students in their setting. Over time, school district educators took increasing responsibility for design, facilitation, and assessment of its collaborative and inquiry-focused approach to professional and organizational learning.

The partnership focused on improving literacy learning and teaching across all grade levels and content areas for a diverse student body. As with all of the Foundation's school district partnerships, poverty, English language learning, and racial and ethnic diversity characterized the student population. Moreover, significant gaps persisted in achievement levels between these and other groups within the student body.

Inquiry #1: Identifying Assets for Student Literacy Learning

The partnership story begins with district educators and stakeholders coming together around the broad issue of how to improve the literacy of the school district's diverse student body. The first phase, or iteration, of the partnership's inquiries into literacy learning and literacy practice involved a district-wide assessment of assets related to student literacy learning. This baseline assessment was part of a broader stakeholder engagement strategy that invited school and school district personnel, parents, and community members to learn about the partnership and to participate in determining focus areas for improving literacy learning and teaching. Over six months, a project team made up of educators in a variety of roles and members of the Ball Foundation team cocreated a series of information-gathering and information-sharing experiences related to the partnership.

Participants in these sessions met in small- and large-group settings to explore factors in their experiences that contributed to powerful learning for them and also to suggest areas of inquiry related to improving literacy for all students. Input from these convenings was compiled and refined to identify several broad areas of inquiry for the baseline assessment. These included educators working collaboratively with one another and with parents, effective instructional practices, and norms of practices and underlying organizational conditions that support student literacy learning.

Next the partners identified a set of indicators of the presence of assets related to these focus areas. The project team did this from two perspectives. The *inside-out* perspective identified the presence of assets in schools, classrooms, and the district that contribute to powerful learning experiences and high levels of student performance. The *outside-in* perspective involved looking to evidence of effective instructional and leadership practices based on research, theory, best practices, and the experience of district educators and Foundation staff. The baseline assessment looked for evidence of the extent to which and ways in which indicators were present in instruction and leadership practices and in the underlying organizational conditions relating to student literacy learning.

Three overarching questions embodied the indicators and framed the baseline assessment:

1. *How do educators and families learn with and from one another to support student literacy learning?* Indicators probed the content of the shared learning experiences and looked for examples of learning venues and formats in which educators and families learned together about classroom literacy practices and home literacy practices.

2. *How do educators and families provide powerful learning experiences for all students?* Indicators probed for instances of differentiating instruction, engaging families as partners in their children's literacy learning, continual

learning among educators and with students and families, and student engagement in purposeful learning.

3. *How do underlying organizational conditions support powerful literacy learning experiences for all students?* Indicators probed for examples of professional learning centered on providing and supporting literacy instruction, as well as examples of school and district-wide values, beliefs, policies, and practices that support literacy learning and teaching.

The project team developed data-collection instruments based on the indicators and created and implemented the process for data collection, including the project team observing classrooms and interviewing teachers and administrators. The baseline assessment also involved surveys of teachers, parents, and students in grades 5–12. Once the data were compiled, the project team was expanded to include a larger representation of district educators who analyzed and interpreted the findings.

As a result of the baseline assessment, the partnership identified three areas for deeper inquiries into literacy learning and teaching: (1) engaging stakeholders across the district in coming to a shared understanding about the meaning, importance, and practice of literacy instruction; (2) developing a strategy for engaging families to support student literacy learning; and (3) fostering greater collaboration between educators in the school district to enhance student literacy learning.

Inquiry #2: Building Collaborative Learning Structures to Support Practice and Student Literacy Learning

As the partnership initiated the baseline assessment, the district began a strategic planning process. The strategies emerging from strategic planning and the focus areas from the baseline assessment came together as a coherent change effort. One point of alignment was the focus area of fostering greater collaboration between educators to enhance student literacy learning and a strategy to transform teaching and learning to ensure the actualization of each student's unique potential (Rowland Unified School District, 2008). These priorities were actualized through the partnership by creating collaborative structures to expand, augment, and connect professional learning across the district.

The baseline assessment revealed that collaborative working and learning opportunities already existed within schools and the school district. The baseline assessment and strategic plan strategy highlighted the need to expand

and connect these opportunities for educators to learn with and from their colleagues from schools across the district. Acting on this need to create expanded, collaborative, and connected educator learning opportunities was the second iteration of inquiries into improving student literacy.

To expand the reach and depth of the partnership, the school district reassigned a principal to lead the district's engagement in the partnership and to work as a liaison between the school district and the Ball Foundation. In addition to funding the liaison position, the Foundation assigned a full-time EI team member who lived in Southern California to work with the liaison to support the growing partnership. In time the school district also assigned a classroom teacher to the partnership's leadership and support structure. Together with their school district colleagues and other members of the Ball Foundation, this group facilitated design, implementation, and assessment of broad, inclusive, and inquiry-based learning experiences centered on improving literacy practices and underlying organizational conditions of literacy learning.

Before the partnership, the district provided and supported a traditional array of professional development opportunities such as supporting attendance at professional meetings and providing site and district workshops focused on instructional methods. The advent of the partnership shifted this pattern of experts transmitting professional knowledge to practitioners. Teachers and other educators in administrative and support roles now participated in design teams with members of the EI team to plan and conduct professional learning experiences. Design teams engaged participants in determining the content and process of their professional learning as they educated themselves about collaborative learning structures such as communities of practice (CoPs) and site leadership teams. Membership on design teams was intentionally rotated among teachers and program, site, and district leaders to build district-wide capacity for designing professional learning experiences.

Building on the focus areas identified through the baseline assessment and the direction suggested by a new strategic plan, the partnership created several collaborative learning structures, or social architectures, to support professional learning and collaboration. Two of these architectures were a district-wide literacy network and CoPs centered on participant-initiated areas of interest related to student literacy learning. In forming the literacy network, the partnership invited educators from across the district who were interested in learning more about literacy teaching and learning to come together around four questions: (1) What are we doing? (shared understanding of goals and outcomes); (2) *How* are we doing it? (understanding of and deepening expertise around shared collaborative practices); (3) How will we know we are doing it? (understanding of and deepening expertise around ways to gather evidence for decision making, including artifacts of student learning); and (4) Who else needs to be in the conversation?

After several convenings of the network during the spring semester, the network matured into multiple CoPs in which groups of educators made a commitment to engage in inquiry together to develop and refine shared practices and to deepen their collective expertise in a specific area related to literacy learning and teaching. Approximately 175 educators joined the literacy network and most participated in a CoP. Some of the focus areas for CoPs included how students learn and the learning conditions that maximize learning; differentiating instruction; literacy instructional strategies; and engaging families to support student literacy learning.

Some CoPs started their inquiries with a focus on theory in a book study format and later moved to application of new ideas and methods. For example, two CoPs focusing on how students learn and conditions that maximize learning undertook a study of brain/mind learning principles put forward by Renate and Geoffrey Caine (Caine, Caine, McClintic, & Klimek, 2009) and applied what they were learning to understanding their own learning processes. The CoP provided a collaborative professional learning structure for application and reflection. Teachers applied their learning in lesson planning, classroom instruction, and examining student work and shared their experiences within the CoP. Principals applied their learning by placing greater attention on professional learning and accomplishing routine information sharing in other ways.

Several CoPs looking at literacy instructional strategies began their inquiries with a focus on practices involving readers and writers workshop (Teachers College, 2010). While they began with workshop methods, participants engaged in further reading, attended workshops, and invited outside consultants into their meetings to delve more deeply into the epistemology underpinning the pedagogy of readers and writers workshop. Participants shared what they were learning and their CoP experiences in a variety of ways at school sites. The network continued to meet several times over the remainder of the partnership to provide opportunities for sharing and connecting learning across CoPs.

Each of the CoPs received guidance and support for framing an inquiry question and structuring an inquiry focused on their question. Facilitators from the Ball Foundation's EI team and the school district provided support for the collaborative inquiries of the CoPs in addition to meetings of the literacy network. This support included protocols for collaborative dialogue and for examining student work; dedicated meeting space with a professional library; a developmental assessment for collaborative inquiries in a CoP; periodically convening together several CoPs with a similar inquiry focus to help them deepen the rigor of their inquiries and learn more about the collaborative inquiry process; and an online networking site dedicated to sharing and connecting learning within the literacy network. CoPs were voluntary and met after school according to their scheduling preferences. Literacy network meetings and multi-CoP meetings took place during the school day. Although CoP members were not compensated for their after-school work time, each CoP received a small stipend to purchase materials related to their focus question. Many of the CoPs continued after the partnership ended.

Inquiry #3: Forging District-Wide Agreements for Highly Effective Instruction

The story of the Ball Foundation's school district partnership concludes with a third iteration of system-wide inquiries into improving student literacy achievement. In the final months of the partnership, district leadership charged a work group with creating a framework of best first teaching practices as a major step toward and milestone of implementing the strategy of transforming teaching and learning. The work group comprising teachers and administrators representing K–12 took on the charge as an inquiry into establishing agreements about highly effective instruction that were based on research. The work group embraced Charlotte Danielson's contention about coming to agreements regarding effective instruction:

> The criteria used to define good teaching must both be grounded in research and reflect the professional wisdom of educators who will use the system. The conversations among educators to establish those criteria can make a substantial contribution to the professional culture of the school. (2007, p. 177)

Several members of the work group had participated in CoPs focused on understanding and applying the brain/mind learning principles put forth by Renate and Geoffrey Caine (Caine et al., 2009). Group members reviewed current research on effective instruction and examined various research-based frameworks of instructional practices. The work group identified teacher and student actions that exemplified sound instruction. As part of its inquiry, the group decided that principles for natural learning identified by the Caines would provide the foundation for the domains of instruction identified in the framework.

The district published the "Framework for Efficacious Instruction" internally as a work in progress with the invitation to educators in the district to contribute to it as they engage in making meaning around it (Rowland Unified School District, 2011). The work group used the term *efficacious* to characterize instruction that makes a difference in student learning. The framework is being used to inform and create a common language about teaching and learning expectations and agreements around the instructional practices that make a difference for student learning. In the current phase of sharing and meaning-making, educators across the district hold conversations face to face and online to unpack the language and descriptors of teacher and student actions. These collaborative experiences are foundational for implementing the improvements in teaching practices described in the framework. Professional learning opportunities provided by the district support personal and collective learning and eventual refinement of the framework to incorporate a broader base of shared understanding and agreements around efficacious or highly effective instruction. The framework can be found online at www.literacyinlearningexchange .org/framework-efficacious-instruction.

Going forward, the district plans to create modules, or learning designs, for sites to use in unpacking each of these five domains: "Developing Teacher Clarity," "Building Democratic Relationships," "Designing for Invested Cognition (Engagement)," "Gathering and Responding to Feedback," and "Developing Expert Learners." Modules will include multisensory experiences and an opportunity for participants to identify actions leading from novice- to master-level instructional practice, a range of developmental progressions called continua. These continua will be used for reflection on instruction both individually and collectively and will be used to create agreements across the district about what a domain looks like in action. Future professional development will integrate the framework with the Common Core State Standards (National Governors Association Center for Best Practices, Council of Chief State School Officers, 2010). The Common Core State Standards are the "what," or content, of instruction and the framework is the "how," or pedagogy.

The three examples of system-wide inquiry related in the story of this school district partnership illustrate a broad and inclusive system-wide approach to collaborative inquiry. Through its inquiries, the school district discovered and built on its instructional and organizational assets and built enduring collaborative work and learning structures to support literacy learning. Chapter 4 further describes the nature and extent of the impact of the Ball Foundation's approach to system-wide collaborative inquiry through the course of this partnership.

It should be noted that this is not a school district with exceptional monetary resources. Quite the contrary. Over the course of the partnership, the school district faced massive cuts in state funding and increased class size and made extensive cuts in personnel and educational support services. What is exceptional about this school district is its openness and commitment to learning and working together to provide and support highly effective instruction for its students.

Creating Conditions for Organizational Learning and Capacity Building

Through its partnerships, the Ball Foundation team and the school districts refined and modeled use of "Design Principles for Organizational Learning and Capacity Building" in creating collaborative, inquiry-based professional learning experiences with the goal of improving literacy for all students. The examples presented in the section "A Tale of Three Inquiries" illustrate how each of the principles shaped partnership learning experiences and actions.

Build shared purpose. Shared purpose comes from forging and enacting agreements for individual and collective action. It provides impetus and direction for action and change. When people see themselves in an organization's purpose, that purpose is a source and referent for action and decision making. The baseline assessment of the partnership discussed in this chapter invited stakeholders across the district into inquiry centered on improving literacy achievement for all students—a large, compelling, and important goal. The literacy network and CoPs invited educators into inquiries of importance to them about improving their instructional and leadership practice as well as the organizational conditions that support student literacy learning. Developing the document "Framework for Efficacious Instruction" led to shared agreements between the work group and to building shared understanding and agreements between all educators in the district.

Access the capacity of stakeholders. Accessing the capacity of stakeholders connects the aspirations, knowledge, skills, and experience of people throughout a school district and enfranchises them in pursuit of shared purpose. Bringing stakeholders together to create shared meaning around the challenges and opportunities within the school district helps people find their connections to the work and one another. Each of the three inquiries brought together people with authority to act and allocate resources, people with information and expertise and diverse perspectives, and those who would be impacted by changing expectations and circumstances brought about as a result of the inquiries. Parents, other community members, and educators participated in the design of the baseline assessment; district educators participated in data analysis and interpretation; all of these stakeholders and students participated in the data collection. The literacy network, CoPs, and development and sharing of the "Framework for Efficacious Instruction" brought teachers, site and district leaders, and others in roles supporting instruction into collaborative inquiries into literacy practice.

Work in systemic ways. When people work in focused and coherent—or systemic—ways, they bring their knowledge and skills to bear from multiple vantage points that enable an organization to adapt and thrive. They not only represent their role and level in a school district, but they also are challenged to look across the district to see a bigger picture—classrooms, schools, and district. The baseline assessment, literacy network, CoPs, and development of the document "Framework for Efficacious Instruction" together focused participants' coherent action on achieving the school district's strategy of transforming teaching and learning. People representing all levels and roles engaged together in building shared understandings and agreements around high-quality instruction. Together the three inquiries represent iterative cycles of planning, action, and reflection that served to generate, share, and connect knowledge.

Work in inquiry-based ways. Organizations that support inquiry-based professional learning cultivate and reinforce an inquiry mindset—a way of thinking that guides behavior and involves being in a learning mode as one acts. An inquiry mindset is more than a desire to learn; it connects learning with action based on new information and reflection. An inquiry mindset seeks more than methods or tools; it seeks deeper understanding of why and under what conditions actions are appropriate and achieve desired results. The three partnership inquiries embodied this inquiry mindset by embedding learning in action and participatory decision making. People came together to learn with and from one another, take action, and reflect and refine practices and conditions of teaching and learning.

Attend to content and process. *How* people do something can be as important as *what* they do. Enacting this belief encourages clarity in why we act, what we do, and how we do it. Shared understanding of process enables an organization to gauge the success of its actions. Each of the inquiries balanced the need for rigorous learning and practice with learning strategies that fostered high energy and engagement. Conversational methods such as World Café (Brown, 2005), Fishbowl (Clark, 2009), and Open Space (Owen, 2007) brought diverse perspectives and voices into conversations that led to shared meaning, agreements, and action. Protocols for conversation such as Process Learning Circles (Caine et al., 2009) enabled CoPs to learn more effectively with and from one another. Protocols for examining student work enabled CoPs to engage in more rigorous and evidence-based inquiries. Overviews of these conversational methods can be found online at www.literacyinlearningexchange.org/technologies-conversation.

Create adaptive solutions. Cocreating solutions to problems builds on the knowledge and experiences of others as an organization works to achieve its purpose and its goals. Multiple iterations of the plan–act–reflect cycle help an organization adapt to its circumstances and changing conditions and to take actions that enable it to thrive. The partnership inquiries brought people together who typically did not interact with one another. Each of the inquiries was designed and facilitated with school district partners representing all levels of schooling and diverse roles. Participating in the design and facilitation of partnership inquiries enabled educators to bring their knowledge and experience into the learning experiences and to build their capacity to design and facilitate learning experiences embodying the design principles for organizational learning and change in their settings.

Build on assets. All school districts have assets—strengths, values, traditions, practices, and accomplishments—to build on. Building on assets encourages a view of problems as possibilities. While not ignoring deficits, focusing on assets provides a place to start problem solving from a position of strength. People are energized when looking for assets. The partnership's baseline assessment was a search for assets that brought people together with energy and commitment that calling people together to fix a problem or plug a deficit will never equal. The literacy network and CoPs helped people find the wealth of assets they could build on when they came together in new ways to discover, learn, and act with shared purpose. The document "Framework for Efficacious Instruction" serves as an example of what is possible when a small group of people tackles an important and compelling task and invites the whole system into making meaning, forging agreements, and enacting them to accomplish something important to everyone.

Conclusion

Moving from group collaborative inquiry approaches to collaborative inquiry as a system-wide capacity-building approach is largely unchartered territory. Examples are few and a theoretical and research base is only beginning to emerge. The work of the Ball Foundation through its school district partnerships offers one approach to taking collaborative inquiry to scale as a means for achieving organizational purpose and goals. Framing the key elements of collaborative inquiry in the Foundation's document "Design Principles for Organizational Learning and Capacity Building" resulted in organizational learning experiences that brought greater focus, coherence, and impact to professional practice and organizational conditions affecting instruction. The partnership story related in "A Tale of Three Inquiries" demonstrates that with intentional design, inquiries large and small can yield important results for schools, for school districts, and ultimately for students.

4

Supporting System-Wide
Collaborative Learning and Practice

Collaborative inquiry as a system-wide capacity-building approach requires a broad and inclusive infrastructure to support educator learning and practice. Research reveals specific collaborative conditions and practices that support educator collaboration and contribute to student learning. Applying these findings through strategies that build the necessary infrastructure for educator learning and practice is key to taking collaborative inquiry to scale.

Chapter 4 identifies research-based conditions and practices that support educator collaboration and professional learning, describes the building of a district-wide infrastructure to support educator collaboration and collaborative inquiry, and presents a model depicting this capacity-building example brought to scale.

Making Collaborative Professional Learning and Practice More Likely and Effective

An infrastructure that supports capacity building makes collaborative practice—collaborative work and collaborative professional learning—more likely and effective. Grounding capacity-building approaches in the premise that all educators serve in roles that provide or support instruction is one way to nurture collaboration and professional learning that is centered on professional practice. This premise guided the three system-wide inquiries presented in the section "A Tale of Three Inquiries" in the previous chapter. Teachers; site, program, and district leaders; and instructional coaches and specialists came together through collaborative inquiries to improve literacy instruction and the conditions and practices in their school district that support effective literacy instruction.

The Ball Foundation's "Framework of Competencies for Professional Practice" (2010c) illustrates the premise that all educators serve in roles that provide or support instruction by outlining collective knowledge, skills, and dispositions for effective literacy instruction as well as practices and conditions that support effective literacy instruction. The competencies speak to the work of teachers (literacy instruction) and to the work of others whose roles impact literacy teaching and learning (support for literacy instruction). Organizational conditions that educators enact together focus, connect, and optimize literacy practices. In the Ball Framework, competencies listed under "Support for Literacy Instruction" and "Organizational Conditions" represent a supportive infrastructure for collaborative professional learning and practice. The excerpt from the Ball Framework presented in Figure 4.1 identifies competencies and organizational conditions for one of the Framework's six areas of literacy practice.

Supporting Collaborative Inquiry

Studies of collaborative inquiry approaches to educator professional learning in the United States and abroad suggest the nature of an infrastructure that supports collaborative educator learning from educator practice. Studies found that making inquiry more intensive, embedded in instructional practice, and yielding student results required sustained support from school and school district leaders. Norms of practice evidenced by the culture of a school district and structural supports specific to collaborative inquiry contributed to its positive impact on instructional practice and student results.

Norms of practice— school district culture	Collaborative work and learning environments (Ball Foundation, 2011; Gallimore et al., 2009)
	Collaborative lesson planning and review of student work (Wylie, Lyon, & Goe, 2009)
	Opportunities for teacher leadership (Ball Foundation, 2011; Nelson & Slavit, 2008)

Figure 4.1. Competencies Related to Providing and Supporting Effective Literacy Instruction

Research-Based Literacy Practices to Differentiate Instruction and Support All Students in Meeting Grade-Level and Content Area Standards	
Literacy Instruction	**Support for Literacy Instruction**
Foundational Knowledge I-1 Know current literacy research in areas pertinent to one's own practice. I-2 Understand how effective literacy practice builds on research-based principles of learning (prior knowledge, cultural background, interest/motivation, and physiological dimensions of memory and cognitive function) in the literacy development of students. I-3 Know when, how, and why to use literacy instructional strategies and assessments. **Actions** I-4 Diagnose student reading problems. I-5 Use informal and formal literacy measures to inform instructional decision making on an ongoing basis. I-6 Apply literacy strategies pertinent to one's own grade/subject area and level of schooling. I-7 Use a wide range of instructional strategies to meet the learning needs of every student. I-8 Differentiate classroom instruction so that *every* student has the opportunity to achieve content standards. I-9 Create pedagogical structures that ensure that students' learning needs are appropriately addressed in the context of classroom instruction. I-10 Work collaboratively to create and adapt literacy practices to meet the learning needs of students.	**Foundational Knowledge** S-1 Know what research says about supporting effective literacy instruction pertinent to one's role. S-2 Understand how effective literacy practice builds on research-based principles of learning (prior knowledge, cultural background, interest/motivation, and physiological dimensions of memory and cognitive function) in the literacy development of students. S-3 Know/anticipate how an innovation will affect curriculum, instruction, and assessment practices (literacy and general curriculum). **Actions** S-6 Provide opportunities and support that enables educators to: • read and critique current research on literacy instruction • acquire and share effective literacy instructional practices • understand and use literacy assessments appropriately • map instructional practices to current research • understand test development and design and relationship to standards and classroom practice S-7 Provide models of and resources for the development of content area instruction in which learners have access to texts at their independent reading level and allow for their interest and prior knowledge to be accessed. S-8 Support new ideas, exploration, and innovation in literacy instruction. S-9 Monitor and report the impact of programs and innovations. S-10 Recruit instructional and support staff who are knowledgeable and skilled in literacy instruction.
Organizational Conditions	
OC-1 Focused and coherent instructional programs and improvement efforts OC-2 Structures that enable educators to work collaboratively to ensure that instruction appropriately supports students' learning needs OC-3 Articulation within and between grade levels, subject areas, and levels of schooling	

	Trust between team members and from principals (Gallimore et al., 2009)
	Work environments where people with different perspectives feel physically and emotionally safe to question current practices and share ideas (Ball Foundation, 2011; Zech et al., 2000)
	Commitment to high-quality instructional practice in the form of transparency, reflection, and rigor (Ball Foundation, 2011)
	Evidence-based decision making (Nelson & Slavit, 2008)
Structural supports	Dedicated time for collaboration and inquiry-based professional learning (Rafferty, 1995)
	Access to timely, meaningful, and useful information about student learning (Gilrane, Roberts, & Russell, 2008)
	Explicit linkages between inquiry-based approaches to professional development and a professional evaluation process that supports inquiry-based professional learning (Sagor, 2000)
	Protocols (Gallimore et al., 2009; Nelson & Slavit, 2008), content experts (Thibodeau, 2008; Timperley & Parr, 2007; Zech et al., 2000), and trained peer facilitators (Gallimore et al., 2009; Zech et al., 2000) to guide the inquiry process
	Opportunities for sharing what educators are learning from their inquiries (Wylie et al., 2009; Timperley & Parr, 2007)

Supporting Collaborative Practice and Professional Learning

Catherine Nelson, in her review of the literature on organizational conditions and practices that lead to improved student learning, found collaboration and collaborative, job-embedded professional learning to be necessary components of changing practice and improving student learning (National Center for Literacy Education [NCLE], 2012b; see also www.literacyinlearningexchange.org/sites/default/files/ncleshortlitreview.pdf). Two large-scale studies cited in Nelson's review further illuminate these findings.

A study by MetLife (2009) revealed a significant difference between US schools and those in high-performing countries. Researchers found that US teachers experience far greater isolation from their colleagues compared to teachers in nations that outperform the United States on international assessments. A second study by McKinsey and Company (Mourshed, Chijioke, & Barber, 2010) probed more deeply into this key difference. School systems around the world that demonstrate consistent improvements in student achievement have in common the practice of teachers sharing and working on their instruction together. In these school systems, collaborative professional learning is integral to and embedded in shared practice. The researchers concluded that collaborative work and collaborative learning are central to improving core education practice and student learning.

Building on the research findings on educator collaboration and professional learning, the National Center for Literacy Education (NCLE) identified six domains, or clusters, of related actions that have the greatest impact on student learning:

- Deprivatizing Practice
- Enacting Shared Agreements
- Creating Collaborative Culture
- Maintaining an Inquiry Stance
- Using Evidence Effectively
- Supporting Collaboration Systemically (NCLE, 2012a)

These actions represent a departure from the conditions of isolated practice reported in the MetLife (2009) and McKinsey (Mourshed et al., 2010) studies. The organizational conditions and practices represented by actions within these six domains describe teachers sharing and working on their practice together, and are indicative of the broad inclusive infrastructure needed for taking education reform to scale, as reported in the RAND study (Glennan et al., 2004). NCLE's "Framework for Capacity Building: Conditions and Practices That Support Effective Collaboration" (2012d) is presented in Figure 4.2.

The organizational conditions and practices outlined in the NCLE Framework are not new. Two factors differentiate the Framework and its related resources from other codifications of effective instruction and leadership practices: (1) their focus on these conditions and practices as an infrastructure to support educator collaborative practice and professional learning from practice; and (2) their focus on capacity building through collaborative inquiry as the means to improving professional practice and student learning.

Figure 4.2. Framework for Capacity Building: Conditions and Practices That Support Effective Collaboration

Domain 1: Deprivatizing Practice
- Formal and informal peer observation occurs regularly.
- All share in the accountability for student learning.
- Adult learning is a shared responsibility.
- Evidence is collected and comfortably discussed with others.
- Learning that occurs through collaboration is captured and shared with others.

Domain 2: Enacting Shared Agreements
- Decision making and actions focus on improving student learning.
- All hold agreements about what quality literacy instruction looks like and about essential outcomes.
- All agree on how to effectively assess essential outcomes.
- Daily work and decision making are driven by these shared agreements.
- Literacy emphasis occurs across content areas.

Domain 3: Creating Collaborative Culture
- Successes and failures are shared safely and without judgment.
- Time for collaboration is used productively and with purpose.
- Participants share the leadership and own the process and outcomes.
- Group members engage in hard conversations.

Domain 4: Maintaining an Inquiry Stance
- Collaborative work has clear goals and purpose.
- Collaboration focuses on the core issues of student learning in our context.
- Intended student outcomes are clearly defined and progress is closely monitored.
- A cycle of plan–act–reflect is used to solve problems of practice.
- Participants commit to acting and reporting back to the group.
- Appropriate expertise is sought when needed.

Domain 5: Using Evidence Effectively
- Collaboration is grounded in evidence of student learning.
- Multiple sources of data are available.
- Participants know how to use data effectively.
- Student work is examined and discussed regularly with others.
- Actions are assessed in terms of impact on student learning.

Domain 6: Supporting Collaboration Systemically
- Dedicated time is provided for professional collaboration within the work week.
- Training, assistance, and tools are provided for effective collaboration.
- Leadership supports and promotes collaborative work.
- Leaders ensure access to timely data sources.
- Experimenting with practice and trying new ideas is encouraged.

In addition to the document "NCLE Framework for Capacity Building" (www.literacyinlearningexchange.org/framework-capacity-building), NCLE offers other resources online to support educators in learning and working on their shared practice: "Building Capacity to Transform Literacy Learning" (NCLE, 2012b) presents a review of research on educator collaboration and professional learning (www.literacyinlearningexchange.org/building-capacity-transform-literacy-learning); "Asset Inventory for Collaborative Teams" (NCLE, 2012a) is designed for inquiry groups to self-assess strengths in the six domains presented in the NCLE Framework (www.literacyinlearningexchange.org/asset-inventory); "Capacity Building Continua" (NCLE, 2012c) offers developmental progressions of key factors within each of the six domains of conditions and practices identified in the NCLE Framework (www.literacyinlearningexchange.org/continua-capacity-building); and the "Remodeling Literacy Learning" (NCLE, 2013) survey report shows a correlation between the routine practice of collaboration among educators, higher levels of trust in a school community, and faster spread of innovative pratices (www.literacyinlearningexchange.org/remodeling).

Building an Infrastructure to Support Collaborative Professional Learning and Practice

Coburn's (2003) four dimensions of scale presented in Chapter 1—spread, depth, shift in ownership, and sustainability—describe the desired outcomes of education reform. While the four dimensions aptly describe the widespread, deep, and lasting changes indicative of taking a change effort to scale, they are not strategies for change. They do not suggest specific actions and conditions that make up the broad, inclusive, and iterative learning experiences and infrastructure to support educator learning and system change called for by the RAND researchers (Glennan et al., 2004). A replicable and scalable approach for capacity building needs to outline broad and inclusive practices for organizational learning and what to look for as evidence of capacity building.

The Ball Foundation's Approach to Organizational Learning and Capacity Building

The Ball Foundation's collaborative, inquiry-based, and system-wide school district partnership approach to capacity building cultivates practices and an underlying organizational structure that support professional collaboration and learning from shared practice. "A Tale of Three Inquiries" in Chapter 3 describes broad and inclusive professional learning experiences framed by the Foundation's "Design Principles for Organizational Learning and Capacity Building." The tale describes system-wide learning experiences that strengthened the school district's infrastructure to support collaborative practice and professional learning.

The Foundation's partnership approach enacts three strategies of organizational learning:

Strategy 1: Support educators in the continual improvement of their shared practice.

Strategy 2: Foster agency and responsibility for practice and student learning.

Strategy 3: Connect people in their shared work.

As it implements these strategies with school district partners, the Foundation looks for three broad indicators, or areas of evidence, of capacity building linked to the domains of conditions and practices described in the NCLE Framework (2012d). The strategies and indicators of the Foundation's capacity-building approach are presented in Table 4.1.

Evaluations conducted by independent evaluators working with the Foundation and the school district examined the extent to which and ways that district educators apply what they are learning through collaborative inquiries (Transfer), take agency and responsibility for their practice and student learning (Ownership), and connect people in their shared work (Connectedness) (Ball Foundation, 2010a). The indicators provide a window into how change evolves, as well as circumstances, or conditions that support or impede change. The Foundation uses the indicators to assess the course of change and the impact of its strategies at several points during the course of a school district partnership (Ball Foundation, 2009, 2010a, 2011)

Table 4.1. The Ball Foundation Partnership Approach to Organizational Learning and Capacity Building

Strategies	Indicators of Capacity Building

Strategy 1: Support educators in the continual improvement of their shared practice.	*Transfer*: people acting on what they are learning
	     Maintaining an Inquiry Stance
	     Using Evidence Effectively

Strategy 2: Foster agency and responsibility for practice and student learning.	*Ownership*: empowerment as a right and responsibility; connecting practice to shared purpose of the district
	     Deprivatizing Practice
	     Enacting Shared Agreements

Strategy 3: Connect people in their shared work.	*Connectedness*: relationships that allow people to be connected to others, knowledge, information, and resources.
	     Creating Collaborative Culture
	     Supporting Collaboration Systemically

Impact: A Supportive Infrastructure for Collaborative Practice

Several themes were apparent from the partnership evaluations for the school district described in Chapter 3 (Ball Foundation 2009, 2010a, 2011). These themes were evident in the structures and processes of daily operations and in the evolution of cultural norms that support collaborative practices and capacity building.

A collaborative inquiry stance or mindset emerged at all levels and scales. This was evident in operations, professional learning, and organizational problem solving and decision making. Educators increasingly cited a focus on issues of student learning, what constitutes evidence of effective practice and student learning, and the power of collaborative approaches. District improvement efforts increasingly engaged educators in collaboratively defining the problems of student achievement, examining evidence, looking to outside expertise, and taking adaptive actions through iterative cycles of planning, action, and reflection. District and site leaders did not carry the burden of improvement alone. Solutions were collaboratively determined, implemented, refined, and assessed. Site leadership teams participated and communities of practice linked their focus to district improvement priorities.

There was increasing "spillover" of collaborative inquiry preferences and approaches. Over time, faculty and district meetings became more collaborative and inquiry focused. Educators became increasingly resistant to outside experts coming into the district and dictating solutions, to "sit and get" workshops, and to having professional learning prescribed for them. They became more skilled at defining student achievement problems and working together to investigate and share what they were learning with their colleagues, and they expected to have the freedom to do so.

Shared ownership of individual and collective practice and student learning was evident in a growing transparency or de-privatization of practice, accountability among educators to one another, empowerment, and shared purpose. Transparency was evident in classroom observations where teachers and site leaders provided feedback and through CoPs and other venues where participants became comfortable with sharing what they were doing in their schools and classrooms and sharing evidence about effects on student learning. Site leadership teams and CoPs offered opportunities for teachers to assume leadership roles for professional learning and practice. Participants in CoPs took leadership of their professional learning rather than rely on district and school leaders to plan and provide that learning. Many educators took leadership roles in designing, facilitating, and assessing professional learning and took initiative to share what they were learning through district convenings, Web seminars, and professional conferences.

Shared agreements and commitments contributed to a growing sense of shared purpose across the district. Through the course of the partnership, the district clarified its priorities and aligned its improvement efforts with a new strategic plan, vision for student learning, and state accountability mandates. As the partnership concluded, district improvement efforts were clearly focused on actualizing the shared agreements represented by the district's "Framework for Efficacious Instruction" document, advancing data literacy among educators, and expanding opportunities for collaboration. Shared and district-wide agreements and common language for expectations for students, effective instructional practices, and the various ways that students demonstrate learning were evident in the district's instructional framework. Formalized commitments to individual and collective actions in classrooms and schools were indicative of shared purpose centered on student achievement and success.

New and revitalized structures emerged that brought educators from all schools, levels, and roles together in professional learning and organizational decision making. Over the past decade, this partnership school district shifted from a primarily site-based to a more centralized focus and direction for instructional and operational leadership. The partnership's organizational approach to capacity building through collaborative inquiry contributed to this shift in several ways. School leadership teams broadened to include greater representation of teachers and others in roles that support instruction, and K–12 school leadership teams participated together in professional learning experiences and problem solving. These multiple team convenings provided a forum for learning and practicing new skills for site leadership. The literacy network and CoPs engaged educators in advancing student literacy. Through school instructional leadership teams and CoPs, participants acquired models and protocols for collaboration and reflective conversations. Over time, educators came to expect that meetings and professional learning would be more collaborative, thereby bringing the voices of teachers and others into decision making.

The professional culture of the school district and specifically the structures of the literacy network, CoPs, and school leadership teams increasingly provided the *safety and encouragement to challenge assumptions about learning and instruction and to take risks and share successes and failures.* Deepening rigor was evident in more systematic use of the plan–act–reflect cycle, examination of student work, and professional conversation, particularly in the district's ongoing focus on differentiating instruction to meet the needs of its diverse student body. District educators spoke often to the importance and growth of trust and respect for others in roles other than their own.

Framing capacity building through collaborative inquiries into shared problems of student learning built shared understandings, agreements, and collective competencies for providing and supporting instruction. Changes in core education practice permeated many school and district functions. The partnership's evaluation findings demonstrate how intentionally centering partnership learning experiences on supporting people in continual improvement of their shared practice, fostering agency and shared responsibility for practice and student learning, and connecting people in their shared work initiated and reinforced organizational conditions and practices to support collaboration and professional learning. Change was widespread, deep, indicative of shared ownership, and suggests the ability to persevere in the face of change and difficult circumstances.

Taking a Capacity-Building Approach to Education Reform to Scale

Figure 4.3 presents a model of the Ball Foundation's partnership approach to taking education reform to scale through its capacity-building approach. Using a variation of the traditional Venn diagram, the model illustrates the work of the partnership through the Foundation's three strategies for organizational learning and capacity building and their impact on educator practice and underlying organizational conditions of teaching and learning represented by Coburn's (2003) four dimensions of scale.

Figure 4.3. The Ball Foundation's Capacity-Building Approach for Taking Education Reform to Scale

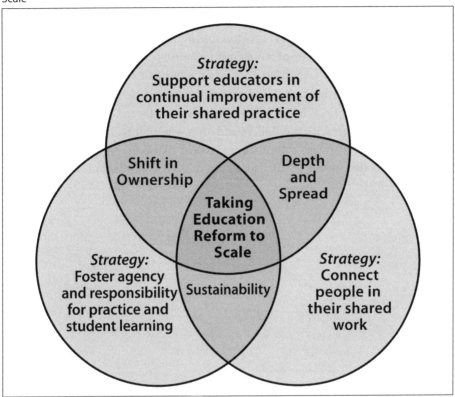

Whereas in a traditional Venn diagram overlap represents that which the three circles have in common, in this variation suggested by Tytel and Holladay (2011), overlap of the circles represents layers of emergence. Here, taking education reform to scale is represented as the emergent phenomena of the impact of the three Ball strategies on a school district's core education practices: depth and spread, shift in ownership, and sustainability.

Through their partnership, the school district and the Ball Foundation brought to scale a collaborative inquiry approach to capacity building. Drawing on the experience and results of the partnership, the proposed model suggests that supporting educators in continual improvement of their shared practice, fostering agency and responsibility for practice and student learning, and connecting people in their shared work make up a scalable approach to building a school district's capacity for continual adaptation and innovation to meet the needs of all students.

Conclusion

Chapters 2, 3, and 4 present collaborative educator inquiry as a viable and scalable capacity-building approach to education reform. Chapter 2 identifies research-based key elements of collaborative inquiry that yield positive student results. Chapters 3 and 4 describe how broad and inclusive inquiry had a deep, meaningful, and lasting impact on instruction, leadership, and the underlying organizational conditions in a midsize urban school district over the course of a five-year partnership with the Ball Foundation. Chapter 5 describes a variation in the traditional plan–act–reflect inquiry cycle that enhances the impact and scalability of collaborative inquiry as an alternative to traditional approaches to education reform.

Scaling Collaborative Inquiry

The challenge of taking education reform to scale is in shifting the routines or patterns of instruction and leadership practice and the underlying organizational conditions that enable all students to succeed. Reform approaches that seek to replicate externally developed methods and structures, and education policies that assume that educators require incentives or sanctions to achieve student results, seldom produce the widespread, deep, and lasting shifts in core education practice required for taking reforms to scale.

Chapter 5 introduces *adaptive action* from the field of human systems dynamics as a variation of the plan–act–reflect inquiry cycle. Collaborative inquiry pursued as adaptive action broadly and inclusively engages educators as groups, faculties, and whole systems in recognizing, understanding, and shifting patterns of practice and organizational conditions to meet the needs of students in their specific settings.

Human Systems Dynamics and Adaptive Action

The field of human systems dynamics (HSD) and the process of adaptive action offer a way of thinking about and engaging in collaborative inquiry that is replicable, scalable, and responsive to meeting the diverse learning needs of students and school and school district contexts.

What Is Human Systems Dynamics?

Several years ago, members of the Ball Foundation's Education Initiatives team became aware of the work of the Human Systems Dynamics Institute (HSDI). Grounded in the fields of chaos theory, nonlinear dynamics, and complexity, and through the pioneering work of its founder, Glenda Eoyang, and a growing network of HSDI associates, the field of human systems dynamics (HSD) studies patterns of behavior, interactions, and decision making in organizations and communities.

According to HSD, emergent patterns are similarities, differences, and conditions that have meaning over space and time (Eoyang & Holladay, 2013). For example, classroom observations reveal similarities and differences in teacher behaviors and student engagement in their learning. Observations of professional meetings and professional development sessions reveal similarities and differences in leadership and how educators engage in professional learning. Similarities and differences in expectations for students, agreements about effective instructional methods, and staff involvement in decision making and planning reveal patterns in the underlying organizational conditions related to learning and teaching.

Identifying patterns is a way of making sense of the outcomes of practice and the influence of underlying conditions. Similarities and differences in student achievement data, for example, reveal trends in overall student achievement and achievement for subgroups of students. Similarities and differences in teacher behavior and student results over time help educators determine practices that best meet student needs in their settings. The same is true when looking for shared practices and conditions in schools where students consistently meet and exceed expectations. Recognizing, understanding, and shifting underlying conditions is a helpful way to examine professional practice, student learning, and systems change.

What Is Adaptive Action?

The Human Systems Dynamics Institute has developed models and methods that enable practitioners to recognize, understand, and set conditions for new patterns to emerge. Adaptive action is one HSD method that educators and others working in organizations and communities are using to improve their practice and achieve results that are important to them. Adaptive action is guided by three questions: *What? So what?* and *Now what?* (Human Systems Dynamics Institute, 2011). Figure 5.1 illustrates the adaptive action cycle.

These straightforward questions inform decision making and action by capturing useful information about existing patterns and by helping participants recognize, understand, and influence underlying conditions and behavior. When applied in iterative cycles, as when educators engage in professional inquiry, participants learn from and act in ways that best fit student needs and their local setting. As they move through the adaptive action cycle, participants ask:

What?	What do we observe? What patterns are present? Where are these patterns present?
So what?	What underlying conditions contribute to the pattern we see? What patterns do we want to change? What patterns do we want to amplify?
Now what?	What actions can we take to shift the patterns? What happened? What patterns are present now?

Figure 5.1. Adaptive Action Cycle

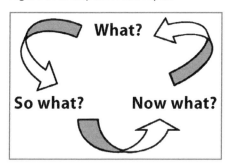

The "So what?" phase of the adaptive action cycle differentiates it from other action-oriented investigative approaches. Actions are predicated on understanding underlying conditions or dynamics that result from multiple actors, different perspectives, and exchanges of information and ideas. "So what?" questions prompt inquirers to uncover and examine assumptions such as agreements around effective instructional practice, optimal learning environments, and the role of families and communities in student learning and success. Considering underlying conditions such as these informs actions taken in the "Now what?" phase of the cycle. By recognizing patterns that have emerged as a result of actions taken through the adaptive action cycle, participants move naturally into successive and iterative cycles of learning from their actions. The following examples illustrate applications of adaptive action in several education contexts.

Applications of Adaptive Action in Education Settings

Adaptive action has been used in communities and organizations around the world to help them achieve results in ways that enable them to be responsive, adaptive, and sustainable. In education settings, adaptive action has been applied in professional learning, project leadership, district planning, and system-wide capacity building. In the first application described in the following sections,

Leslie Patterson, codirector of the North Star of Texas site of the National Writing Project, describes using the adaptive action cycle as a frame for teacher inquiry and for organizing Writing Project site work. In the second application, Royce Holladay, director of the HSDI Network, describes adaptive action as a process for planning and documenting work in a federal grant project. Barbara Iversen, a member of the Ball Foundation's Education Initiatives team, describes how adaptive action reframed traditional school district planning. The fourth and last application describes a district-wide intervention using adaptive action as a means for building the school district's capacity to provide and support highly effective instruction.

Adaptive Action: Teacher Inquiry as Adaptive Action at the North Star of Texas Writing Project

The National Writing Project (NWP) website (www.nwp.org) claims that, since its inception in 1974, more than 70,000 teacher-leaders have taught an additional 1.2 million teachers. At the core of this resilient professional development network is the absolute commitment to teacher inquiry—teachers learning from one another and from their students. NWP is a generative professional learning network driven by inquiry.

The North Star of Texas Writing Project in the Dallas–Fort Worth area has prepared more than 180 teacher-leaders in the past nine years, and those teachers have worked with hundreds of their colleagues in schools throughout Texas. They have wholeheartedly adopted NWP's central focus on inquiry, which might look a bit different at each of the almost 200 NWP sites across the country. At the North Star site, educators use adaptive action to frame individual and collective inquiries. They began by using the adaption action cycle questions—*What? So what?* and *Now what?*—as the frame for teacher inquiry in individual classrooms.

In their classroom research, network members used multiple cycles of adaptive action to replace the more familiar (and more linear) five-step research process: statement of problem, review of literature, methodology, findings, and conclusion (Patterson, Wickstrom, Roberts, Araujo, & Hoki, 2010). The teachers explored "What?" was happening with their students by examining student work, standardized test scores, student comments, their anecdotal records, and other relevant data for patterns (meaningful similarities and differences). As they made sense of what they were seeing, these educators reflected on "So what?" it all meant in terms of possible influences on the students' learning, the constraints and supports in the school context, and the potential contributions of various instructional approaches. They asked questions about what instructional support would best help students become independent and strategic readers and writers—in other words, "What kinds of support do students need to become literate? When should teachers step in and offer more support? When should teachers step out and let students function independently?" (L. Patterson, personal communication, July 31, 2012).

At this point, teachers were ready to focus on "Now what?" as they framed a specific research question and decided on an instructional approach and how they might document student responses. Their implementation of this plan initiated another cycle, and, as they documented their students' responses, tried to make sense of what they were seeing, and adjusted their instruction accordingly, they cycled through those three questions again and again. Those questions then provided a structure as they wrote up their findings to share with colleagues. According to Patterson, the project's codirector, "Adaptive Action is a great fit for teacher inquiry because, just like great teaching, it is recursive, flexible, and allows for the unpredictable. More important, the *"So What?"* step makes space for deep reflection and critical thinking about the implications of our instructional actions" (L. Patterson, personal communication, July 31, 2012).

Adaptive action is foundational to the North Star site's approach to teacher inquiry, but they have also integrated it into other aspects of their Writing Project work to scale their inquiry process to larger site activities. They have used the three questions to organize their leadership meetings, to structure professional development workshops, and to report on their work at professional conferences. They have also used it to structure a statewide collaborative research project funded by NWP. Patterson notes, "We find Adaptive Action useful at various points in our work. In other words, we use those three questions as we plan, as we are in the midst of a challenging issue, and as we look back and report on our work to others. Those three questions, and the complex inquiry/ action orientation that they represent, are now embedded in the culture of this community of practice, the North Star of Texas Writing Project" (L. Patterson, personal communication, July 31, 2012).

Adaptive Action in Project Leadership

Several years ago, Royce Holladay, director of the Human Systems Dynamics Institute Network, consulted with a large urban school district in Minnesota that had received a federal Safe Schools/Healthy Students grant that encompassed a number of projects. Holladay taught the adaptive action cycle to the project leaders so they could use it in planning and in documenting their work.

One of the project leaders was in charge of school social workers. His project was to build a partnership with county children's mental health professionals to provide mental health services for students and families on school campuses. The project was highly successful and sustained itself over time (Sander, Everts, & Johnson, 2011).

A couple of years after working with this director in the grant project, Holladay found herself working with the director on a different project, and she asked him what he believed contributed to the success of the partnership between the school district and the county agency, a relationship that traditionally is fraught with challenges around funding, data control, privacy issues, and "turf" concerns. The director stated that early on he and the director of the county mental health professionals used several of the HSDI models and methods to arrive at agreements about their work together and to build and implement their partnership in ways that would be sustainable. The director stated that as they worked together, they consistently used the adaptive action cycle to frame their questions, to identify where they were in the process, and to see what they needed to do next.

When they came up against challenges to be overcome and boundaries to be crossed, they stopped to look at the patterns they wanted to shift and talked about how best to approach them. For instance, they needed to find ways to share student and client data across the boundaries that separated their systems. They needed to blend or access funding streams that included categorical requirements and regulations. They needed to have a program flexible enough to serve multiple and different needs even as it developed a strong, resilient foundation. Starting early in their relationship, these two leaders came to understand the challenges from the other's perspective and developed a set of shared assumptions. First, money questions had to be laid out on the table; they knew there could be no secrets or second-guessing about fiscal issues and challenges. Second, they agreed to a process for data sharing that both agencies perceived as viable and confidential. Third, they agreed that neither individual would stand alone in their partnership; they would support each other in taking credit and being accountable for whatever emerged.

At each challenge, they used the adaptive action cycle first to describe the current state of affairs: Who was doing what? What was needed? What data or information did they have? They then used that information to understand their situation and identify the implications of each option they saw for taking action. Finally, they put those steps into action and watched for outcomes. For example, when making decisions about shared staff in their colocated clinics on school sites, they had to consider the principal's accountability for the children in the school, the accountability of the county for overseeing the work of paid staff, and the concerns that a noneducator might face in a workplace with a more traditional educational culture. As they considered the impact of such an arrangement, the partners worked with the staff and principals involved to establish some basic expectations, and then they allowed for individual adaptations, based on the specific needs at each site. Over time, they conducted periodic checks to be sure the arrangements and relationships were working. When they hit rough spots, they went back to the three adaptive action questions to understand what was happening, what their options were, and what actions provided the greatest leverage for moving forward.

The codirectors worked to build adaptive capacity into their work so that the structures and agreements were flexible enough to be sustainable over time. The partner from the school district was convinced that they had been so successful because, over time, they had continued to adapt and respond through the adaptive action cycle of questions. Almost ten years after the inception of this project, the resulting programs have grown to multiple campuses, and hundreds of children and families have been served. Both the county agency and the school district have been able to meet their categorical requirements for funding, data sharing, and confidentiality. Staff who work in and support the in-school mental health clinics have found ways to work in these new relationships and to solve problems together to serve the children and families who need their help (Holladay, personal communication, July 19, 2012).

Adaptive Action Planning: An Alternative to Strategic Planning

Recently, Barbara Iversen a member of the Ball Foundation EI team, consulted with a former Foundation partner school district in Illinois to support district planning. Iversen modeled and used the adaptive action cycle with a vertical team representing executive leadership, program leaders, and the community to establish a broad purpose for the work of the school district (Iversen, personal communication, August 13, 2012). She used a variation of the adaptive action framing questions to guide the planning process (Human Systems Dynamics Institute, 2011):

> **What is important here?** and **What is our work?** What is happening in the school district? How are students performing? How are adults and students affected? How do people spend their time? How are parents and the community engaged in the school district and their local school?
>
> **What would we expect to see people doing and hear people saying to make our purpose a reality?** What are the patterns in the data and what we observe? What shapes those patterns? What are the conditions that currently exist in the school district and what do they mean to student

learning? The actions of adults? What do the data and our observations say about the gap between where we are and where we want to be? What does this tell us we should do? What strategies would be effective to move us forward?

What action do we commit to in order to move the district, schools, teams, and grade levels toward our purpose? What conditions do we need to establish to move forward? What actions will we take to create new patterns of interaction, performance, and decision making? How will we share and connect what we learn?

Iversen repeated the process with the superintendent's cabinet, department of instruction, principals, representatives from school leadership teams, and family and community engagement groups. Each member of these groups also answered the questions for him- or herself. In turn, these participants repeated and led the process at school sites and within departments or functions to focus and connect individual and collective actions.

Once the groups answered the guiding questions, they found themselves back at the "What?" stage, asking what difference their actions made, determining their readiness for moving forward or the need to backtrack to change their approach to bring about a greater shift in the patterns they observed. The adaptive action framing questions created space for recognizing and understanding patterns, making small shifts in actions or conditions, and critically reflecting on patterns that emerge from these shifts. Glenda Eoyang's contrast between traditional strategic planning and adaptive action planning—taking immediate action based on feedback, gathering relevant data about consequences, and then considering subsequent action—provides for feedback, gathering relevant data about consequences, and then considering subsequent action, and it provides flexibility and adaptability not present in more traditional strategic planning approaches (Human Systems Dynamics Institute, 2011, p. 2).

The school district's board of education sought a planning process that would yield actionable direction rather than a plan of ideas, and a process that would enable them to monitor progress toward the school district's goals. Through adaptive action, the school district broadly and inclusively moved toward achieving the direction set by the vertical team. A valued and limited resource of a school district—how people use their time together—was shifted to focus on ongoing inquiries, framed by adaptive action, into practices and conditions of teaching and learning. Meetings increasingly focused on questions relating to providing highly effective instruction for all students, what served as evidence of student results, and continual improvement of practice and organizational conditions to support learning and teaching.

Adaptive Action for District-Wide Capacity Building

Over the 2011–12 school year, several members of the Ball Foundation Education Initiatives team and the HSD Institute collaborated in a capacity-building partnership with a midsize urban school district in the California Bay Area. During the course of the partnership, members of the EI team and the HSD Institute modeled and taught HSD models and methods to ninety educators, approximately 15 percent of the district staff representing all levels, roles, and functions of the school district. Central to this effort was teaching and supporting educators in using adaptive action.

The goals of the partnership were to increase the school district's capacity for highly effective instruction with a focus on collaborative practice, professional learning, and instructional coherence. The partnership was designed to provide iterative educator learning experiences through which they would apply adaptive action to investigate and work to resolve "sticky issues," or persistent problems related to instruction, supporting instruction, or conditions surrounding teaching and learning. As this was the first collaboration between the Ball Foundation and the HSD Institute in a system-wide intervention, the organizations were also investigating the usefulness of HSD models and methods, particularly adaptive action, to educators in teaching, instructional coaching, and leadership roles for investigating and resolving issues of importance to them.

Through the course of the partnership, participants cited using and / or experiencing others using adaptive action in site leadership meetings, whole-school staff meetings, district meetings, and meetings involving teachers and literacy coaches. Issues included instruction, collaboration, leadership, conflict resolution, and communication. Most participants noted that it took several cycles of adaptive action to clearly understand the multiple factors contributing to the patterns they observed. Participants also noted that resolving issues benefited from explicit coaching or at least informal conversation with a fellow participant (Ball Foundation, 2012b, 2012c).

Several themes emerged from interviews conducted as part of the partnership's evaluation. The themes are supported by the voices of teachers, site and district leaders, and an instructional coach (Ball Foundation, 2012a).

> **Shared language and approach to seeing, understanding, and taking action on what participants observed as patterns**
> I think [a] . . . helpful idea out of HSD is the idea about patterns and influ-

encing patterns rather than accomplishing a goal. And I think that's been a useful mind shift for me in my work. I think sometimes principals want to fix everything and solve everything and if you haven't closed the achievement gap and gotten your scores to every child being proficient, you're a failure. And I think for me—not that you don't keep working towards that end—you see patterns more clearly and your ability to influence patterns of behavior as a means to that end, rather than "This is a program we're going to implement" or "This is what we're going to do." So I appreciate that. I think that's been a useful kind of thinking shift for me. (Secondary principal)

I think that one of the things that resonated the most for us collectively was really putting that focus into just thinking about things differently and what happens if we make a little shift here and a little shift there. How might that change and impact things? And I think it's helped all of us, but it's especially helped me move away from thinking that I have to have a whole theory and model in place in order to implement change. Maybe the change is just a little push or a little pull or a little this or a little that.…[Now I feel as though I have] the permission to think in some smaller bites that can become bigger. (District administrator)

Giving people options and confidence in taking action to shift patterns

I use recognition of patterns with my students to let them understand that these are the patterns we're seeing, and ask them: "What can we do to change these patterns?" So I give the students a little more input and responsibility into the classroom environment. And I use that as a part of how I take care of classroom management. I've looked at how HSD models could be used within the classroom to promote those behaviors that you want to see and change the patterns without the punitive or consequential kind of actions that usually happen due to behavior in a classroom. So I would say that it has affected my management skills as a teacher, it's affected my leadership skills as a teacher-leader, affected my own personal skills as a father, a husband, and those kinds of things because it kind of permeates everything that you do. (Elementary teacher)

I was thinking, "Oh, I haven't been using the [HSD] language." Then I realized it just becomes a natural part of what you do. I am going to give some examples. I think the biggest part has been the reminder to stand in inquiry for myself and then to foster that in the teachers that I work with through my coaching role. I think that has grown, because at first it was mostly about myself and now it's asking the questions—*What?, So what?, Now what?*—with small groups of teachers or one-on-one with teachers. So it actually changed my interactions with teachers overall and I think strengthened them because when you work as a coach, the perception is often you're coming in as an expert, even though I say I'm not. We're learning together, we're growing together. They still want answers. So being able to ask the questions and look at patterns together and see where we can [shift them] and look for the difference that's going to make a difference in things (not using that language, of course) has been my focus now with teachers. And it's naturally developed. In the beginning of the year, they were saying things like "Come on; don't put it back on me; just give me the answers." And now they know the cycle we're going to go through. They know this is what we do now.…We do a cycle of inquiry. We ask questions and work together and it's not this … top-down type of thing [where] "I'm an expert and you're going to learn from me." So that's been great. (Literacy coach)

Fostering an inquiry stance or mindset of active learning and reflective practice

What I found [using adaptive action in my classroom] was that they were like mini-actions. Everything I do now I look at as a puzzle. So if I give a math test and a kid doesn't do well on fractions, instead of saying, "This kid doesn't know this," I'll reflect on what I've been teaching. Where did this go, what went wrong for this kid? Something happened? And then I will think about if this is what happened, what inputs would I need to first of all diagnose the problem so I really understand it and then, what will I do, how will I intervene to help get the outcomes that the kid and I both want? That process I do constantly. . . . I'm getting better [at noticing the] huge amounts of information that you can get just by watching. And then as I reflect on the day, I ask myself what were the patterns I was seeing in the way kids were engaging? And then what patterns do I want to see? And then what kind of suggestions, what things can I do the next day? So for instance, I let the kids choose where they want to sit on the floor, but if I see a kid that's disengaged, or a group of kids that's disengaged, I'll invite them to the front. So at the beginning I'll say, "Oh, so I haven't talked to you guys at all. Why don't you three come sit around?" So adaptive action and thinking about inputs and outcomes has become second nature for me in the classroom. (Elementary teacher)

I think that I am more mindful of trying to create lessons and opportunities and structures that encourage inquiry. It's a challenge because a lot of times kids look at teachers and want us to be the masters. We have all the answers. And sometimes the answer is to go find it yourself. And so I think they're developmentally more comfortable with inquiry because that's really what it's all about for them. But also I think that by creating structures in the classroom through the presentation of content and the kinds of requirements within set assignments, inquiry becomes much more evident. (Secondary teacher)

Success in the four diverse applications of adaptive action—teacher professional learning, project leadership, school district planning, and system-wide capacity building—illustrates how adaptive action can lead to deep, widespread, and meaningful changes in collaborative work and professional learning. Through adaptive action, teachers, administrators, program leaders, instructional coaches, and others in roles that support instruction became more adept at recognizing and understanding patterns of behavior, interactions, and decision making, which in turn made them more adaptive and responsive to student needs.

Collaborative Inquiry as Adaptive Action

Educator inquiry is typically represented as a cycle of iterative episodes of planning, action, and reflection through which participants strive to answer a question or resolve a problem of importance to them. Applications of the key elements of collaborative inquiry presented in Chapter 2 vary in the literature and research. Variations include the focus or scope of inquiries, levels and roles of participants, and use of protocols for reflection and sharing new learning. Repeated cycles of planning, action, and reflection characterize the professional inquiry process.

Some treatments of educator inquiry emphasize the consideration of current practices, organizational conditions, and student learning behaviors and achievement before initiating the plan–act–reflect cycle (Bray, Lee, Smith, & Yorks, 2000, p. 13; Stringer, 2007). This attention to observing and understanding current circumstances prior to planning is consistent with the "What?" and "So what?" questions of adaptive action. Placing greater emphasis on observing before planning and acting helps participants more clearly understand the student learning problem that focuses the inquiry, as well as identify actions, underlying conditions, and student characteristics that may contribute to the problem. Recognizing and understanding practice and conditions enables educators to more intentionally focus their actions and to reflect on the consequenc-

Figure 5.2. Adaptive Action and the Inquiry Cycle

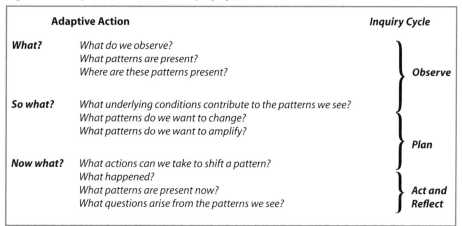

es of their actions and the conditions that affect student learning. Approaching inquiry in this way more strongly links reflection on the impact of previous actions and conditions to successive inquiry cycles. This applies to individual, group, and system-wide approaches to educator inquiry. Figure 5.2 illustrates the adaptive action framing questions, placing greater attention on observing and understanding current patterns of practice, organizational conditions, and student learning as they engage in the plan–act–reflect cycle.

Approaching inquiry in this way moves participants to successive and iterative cycles of learning from action by bringing attention back to observation as educators reflect on their actions. The "Now what?" phase of one inquiry initiates the "What?" phase of a subsequent inquiry cycle. The application examples illustrate this recursiveness and its value to the work described in each application.

The four applications of adaptive action in education settings discussed in the preceding sections are group and system-wide examples of collaborative inquiry. In the Writing Project application, teachers used successive cycles of adaptive action to hone their inquiry focus, determine appropriate instructional approaches, and document student results. Making a greater effort to recognize patterns, contributors to patterns, and small actions that might shift patterns in constructive ways led participants to informed and intentional actions and provided a way for teachers to understand their impact. In the project leadership and planning applications, leaders used successive cycles of adaptive action to clarify their understanding of issues and to recognize patterns in data, behavior, interactions, and decision making in order to identify where they were in the process of managing, planning, and understanding results. Educators in the system-wide application found that cycling through successive and iterative cycles of adaptive action allowed them to clarify persistent and seemingly intractable problems by enabling them to recognize patterns, take small actions, and look for patterns in results.

The system-wide collaborative inquiry approach presented in Figure 5.3 presents inquiry as broad, collaborative, and applicable at all levels and scales in a school district. The approach depicts the plan–act–reflect cycle of professional inquiry framed by the adaptive action questions. Approaching inquiry in this way offers several advantages. Focus on the "Observe" phase encompassing "What?" and "So what?" helps participants to recognize and understand patterns of practice, underlying conditions, and student learning before they formulate a specific inquiry plan and move on to action. The "Act and Reflect" phase directly links action with reflection on the results of action to encourage deeper understanding of actions and their implications, thereby moving the participants in subsequent actions to amplify desired results or patterns through successive iterations of adaptive action.

Enhancing the Power and Scalability of Collaborative Inquiry through Adaptive Action

Collaborative inquiry framed by adaptive action fosters the deep and rigorous investigations of practice envisioned by John Dewey (1933) in his call for "reflective thinking" described in Chapter 2 and by Richard Elmore (1996) in his call for professional learning centered on "core education practice" presented in Chapter 1. Both scholars stress the need for educators to understand the nature of knowledge, how students learn, and how this knowledge manifests in education practice and impacts student learning.

Building capacity system-wide to provide and support instruction that meets the needs of every student is at the heart of the challenge of bringing education reforms to scale. Capacity-building approaches that enact the key elements of collaborative inquiry through broad and inclusive adaptive action can meet this challenge. Table 5.1 illustrates how collaborative inquiry approached in this way builds the capacity of educators and systems of educators to adapt, innovate, and respond to student needs in their settings.

Collaborative inquiry as adaptive action is supported by a series of templates that guide system-wide, practice-based, iterative professional and organizational learning. The templates are available in Appendix B, as well as online at www.literacyinlearningexchange.org/adaptive-action-templates.

Figure 5.3. Collaborative Inquiry as Adaptive Action

Observe

What do we observe? What patterns are present? Where are these patterns present? What underlying conditions contribute to the patterns we see?

Why is this student learning problem important and meaningful to us?

What evidence (patterns in data, observations, student work samples) describes the student learning problem?

What underlying conditions contribute to the patterns we see:

> *(1) assumptions about students, student learning, and effective instructional practices we hold and enact individually and collectively?*
> *(2) agreements about effective instruction and conditions that support learning and teaching?*

Who else has a stake in or responsibility for resolving the student learning problem?

How is resolving the problem related to our school or district priorities?

What actions have been taken previously to resolve the student learning problem?

What happened? What's working/not working? In what circumstances were previous actions successful? How do we know?

What else do we need to know to help us understand the student learning problem and how others have attempted to resolve it?

Plan

What patterns do we want to change? What patterns do we want to amplify? What actions can we take to shift a pattern?

What will each of us commit to learn about, try, and share with others in our inquiry group?

When will we take these actions?

What resources (time, information and other data, input from others) will we need?

How will we capture our learning?

How will we know that our actions are on course for improving student learning?

What will we look for as evidence of the impact of our actions on student learning?

What will we look for as evidence of underlying conditions that support learning and teaching?

Act and Reflect

What happened? What patterns are present now? What questions arise from the patterns we see?

What happened as we tried new methods? How do we know?

What patterns of student performance and learning behaviors do we observe?

What did we learn about conditions that support instruction and student learning?

How has what happened confirmed or challenged:

> *(1) our assumptions about students?*
> *(2) agreements about effective instructional practices within our group? Our school? Our district?*
> *(3) the findings of others?*

What are we doing differently based on what we learned?

What questions arise from what we learned?

What additional information/data do we need to support further inquiry?

How might what we learned inform school or school district priorities?

How will we share our learning with others beyond our inquiry group?

Table 5.1. Scaling Collaborative Inquiry

Key Elements of Collaborative Inquiry	Guiding Questions of Collaborative Inquiry as Adaptive Action	Implications for Scaling
Investigate shared questions or problems of practice.	What actions have been taken previously to resolve the student learning problem? What happened? What's working/not working? In what circumstances were previous actions successful? How do we know? Why is this problem important and meaningful to us? How is solving this problem related to our school/district priorities?	Meaning and importance of the question/problem to participants and the school/district How broadly the question/problem is held Likelihood that the question/problem will challenge assumptions about students, their learning, and effective instructional and leadership practices, and underlying conditions affecting teaching and learning
Learn with and from colleagues.	Who (else) has a stake in or responsibility for resolving the student learning problem? What will each of us commit to learn about, try, and share with others in our inquiry group?	Participation of teachers, site/district/program leaders, and others in roles supporting instruction Participation of those who have a stake in solving the problem and those whose work could be affected by its resolution
Seek expertise and perspectives of others.	What else do we need to know to help us understand the student learning problem and how others have attempted to resolve it? What underlying conditions—assumptions about students, student learning, and effective instructional practices we hold and enact individually and collectively, and agreements about effective instruction and conditions that support learning and teaching—contribute to the patterns we see?	Inclusion of others who hold expertise related to the question/problem, may see the issue or problem differently, or who have grappled with it previously Consideration of research, theory, and practices others have found effective
Use evidence and data.	What evidence (e.g., patterns in data, observations, student work samples) describes the student learning problem? What will we look for as evidence of the impact of our actions on student learning? What will we look for as evidence of underlying conditions that support learning and teaching?	Multiple sources of data about students, their performance, and organizational conditions that support teaching and learning Recognition and understanding of patterns in data, observations, and student work
Act, reflect, and refine practice.	How has what happened confirmed or challenged (1) our assumptions about students? (2) agreements about effective instructional practices? (3) the findings of others? What patterns of student performance and learning behaviors do we observe? What questions arise from what we learned?	Patterns in student learning behaviors and results related to actions taken as part of the inquiry Actions participants will take to amplify desired patterns and diminish others Subsequent actions and their impact
Share and connect learning.	How will we share our learning with others beyond our group? How might what we learned inform school or district priorities?	Connections made between inquiries and inquirers Publication of inquiry findings Invitations to others in subsequent iterations of inquiries/adaptive actions

The guiding questions of collaborative inquiry framed by adaptive action support collaborative work and collaborative professional learning; build on prior knowledge; uncover underlying assumptions about students, their learning, and what constitutes effective instruction; and connect professional learning within and across schools. Pursued broadly and inclusively as adaptive action, collaborative inquiry fosters the deep and consequential changes in education practice and conditions of teaching and learning required to truly scale education reform.

Conclusion: Collaborative Inquiry as a Scalable Alternative to Traditional Approaches to Education Reform

Reform efforts challenge but seldom alter core practice and the underlying conditions of schooling. After spending decades—and billions of dollars—on education reform, we still have far too many children left behind, largely because the idea of taking reforms to scale has too often relied on the replication of externally developed methods. Researchers, scholars, and organizations supporting reform challenge this limited view of change and what it means to take change to scale. Capacity-building approaches that broadly and inclusively engage educators in collaboration and inquiry-based professional learning are challenging what Richard Elmore (1996) refers to as "the core of education practice" and producing results in student performance.

Research findings attribute increased overall student achievement and increased achievement of traditionally low-performing students to educator collaboration and professional learning in the context of shared practice. Studies of inquiry approaches reveal that when educators (1) investigate shared problems of student learning with colleagues through iterative cycles of action and reflection; (2) draw on data, other evidence, expertise, and multiple perspectives; and (3) share and connect what they learn with other educators, their actions yield positive student results. When inquiries include teachers and others in roles that support instruction such as site and district leaders, instructional coaches, and district program leaders, professional knowledge is shared more broadly within and across schools.

A comprehensive study of reforms successfully brought to scale in schools and districts in the United States and abroad found educators learning from their practice, as well as school and district infrastructures that support educator learning and system change, to be key factors in achieving widespread, deep, and consequential change. Michael Fullan's (2011) call for capacity-building approaches to reform extends these findings by calling for education policies and school district practices that encourage building collective capacity to adapt and respond to student learning needs.

Studies link system-wide approaches to collaboration and educator inquiry with increased transfer of what educators learn to changes and greater coherence in instruction, leadership, and organizational conditions within and across schools. Schools and school districts that embrace collaborative inquiry approaches to professional and organizational learning demonstrate strong evidence of educators taking ownership of continual improvement in providing and supporting instruction and student achievement, as well as evidence of connecting people in their shared work.

In addition to fostering new methods of instruction and approaches to leadership, system-wide collaborative inquiry approaches such as those described in the applications of adaptive action in Chapter 5 reveal evidence of habits of mind that contribute to improved practice and student results. Educators increasingly question *how*, *why*, and *under what conditions* new methods contribute to positive student results. Educators demonstrate increased self-efficacy, attributing student results to teaching and leadership practice rather than external causes; they exhibit greater ownership of and accountability for shared practice and student learning; and they are more receptive to new ideas. When educators collaborate and learn together through iterative cycles of observing, acting, and reflecting on patterns of practice and patterns of student learning, they build individual competencies and increase their schools' and school districts' capacity to adapt, innovate, and respond to meet the needs of their students.

Several aspects of a system-wide approach to collaborative inquiry as presented in this book contribute to it being a scalable alternative to traditional approaches of education reform:

System-wide collaborative inquiry begins and functions "at scale." It applies within and across all levels of schools, teams, departments, and functions. It supports investigations involving many participants and far-reaching issues, and it supports smaller and more focused inquiries of teams or groups. It guides inquiries focused on instruction, leadership, and underlying conditions of learning and teaching. It supports professional learning, and it serves decision making, problem solving, and school and district improvement efforts. It allows for starting anywhere in the organization and connects participants and new learning. Participants need never get stuck. The inquiry cycle framed by adaptive action generates more questions that take participants into deeper investigation and continual adaptation in responding to local needs.

System-wide collaborative inquiry changes the ways that district and site leaders participate in education reform. The literature of education reform calls for leaders to be knowledgeable and supportive advocates for change. As described in the examples presented in this book, system-wide inquiry calls for leaders to be advocates *and* to be actively engaged in inquiries with other educators as co-inquirers and cocreators of professional knowledge and solutions to problems affecting student learning. Their broad perspective and stake in solutions, their ability to access and allocate time and funding to collaboration and professional learning, and their potential to focus and bring coherence to professional learning and improvement efforts are significant contributors to the impact and sustainability of reform efforts.

System-wide collaborative inquiry is practical and cost effective. It is not front-loaded with new language or methods. Participants learn naturally through pursuing their interests, commitments, and need to know. The language of system-wide inquiry is simple and the cycle of adaptive action is easily explained and readily learned. System-wide inquiry approaches shift the expenditures for professional learning and change from mass purchases of new programs, materials, and outside experts to buying time for educators to work and learn together and create reforms that best fit the needs of their students in the context of their schools and school district.

Through capacity-building approaches such as system-wide collaborative inquiry, we are learning that knowledge and expertise are already in the room, as are ways for accessing and building on that knowledge and expertise. We are learning that meaningful change happens when educators take responsibility for shared practice and investigate and determine solutions together. We are learning that how we work and engage with others in professional learning is a major factor in the results for our schools and our students.

Decades of reform driven by policies assuming that educators need to be incented or coerced into improvement and reform approaches that import "best practices" have produced disappointing and unacceptable student results. It is time for an alternative—an alternative that broadly and inclusively brings educators together and supports them in learning with and from one another as they investigate shared problems of student learning and determine solutions that best fit their students and their settings.

Appendix A

The Ball Foundation Design Principles for
Organizational Learning and Capacity Building

Grounding Fields of Knowledge			
Human/Adult Learning *Research-based principles of learning and learning characteristics and preferences of adults*	**Organizational Learning** *Theories and practice around capacity building and methods for engaging people in whole systems change*	**Systems and Complexity** *Implications from the sciences of chaos, complexity, and living systems*	**Ball Foundation Experience** *Assumptions based on Ball's partnership experience*

Beliefs	Principles	Implications for Design and Practice
• We must be the change that we want to see in the world. • People and organizations are capable of creating their preferred future. • You cannot transfer your energy for learning to others; you can only tap into their energy. • Learning is done in the context of our humanity and the world around us. • Organizations are living systems capable of learning, creating, making meaning, and self-organizing. • Complex organizations change when they engage with new information and new relationships. • Learning organizations provide the conditions for adaptive, systemic, and generative change to happen. • In learning organizations, leadership is distributed; collaboration is the way of doing business; and decision making is shared by all stakeholders. • Design allows a system to live and emergence to happen. • Literacy is the cornerstone of learning and a gateway to empowerment. • We can move from classrooms and schools that are islands of excellence, the current reality, to a system of schools that ensures high achievement for every student.	***Build shared purpose***	Bring people together to discover what they really care about, to determine their highest aspirations for students and themselves, and invite them into something larger than themselves.
	Access the capacity of stakeholders	Engage staff, students, parents, and community members in learning about the school district, sharing what is important, and making choices about what is best for schools and the district.
	Work in systemic ways	Engage people in ways that help them achieve what is important to the school district by gaining access to one another and to information and seeing interconnections between grade levels, subject areas, schools, families, neighborhoods, processes, and relationships.
	Use inquiry to guide practice	Bring people together in dialogue, learning, and reflection where they ask questions that matter, make their practice visible to others, seek relevant information and data, and plan and implement actions with ongoing reflection and feedback.
	Attend to content and process	Create learning processes that engage people in making meaning and finding connections between information, people, and situations.
	Create adaptive solutions	Cocreate with partners ways to acquire, share, and use information that generate new relationships and connections to solve problems.
	Build on assets	Identify and build on strengths, values, traditions, practices, and accomplishments.

Conditions That Support Organizational Learning and Capacity Building

- Participants have the authority to make substantive recommendations, decisions, or plans about the work.
- Key stakeholders—those with authority, access/control over resources, expertise, information, and need—engage at all levels of the work.
- Leaders see themselves as learners.
- District and school leaders actively engage in the work (codesign of processes, sponsorship, participation, and follow-through).

- Participants see the need for others' contributions and willingly work together.
- Communication between partners is open and unfettered.
- Work continues in between formal partnership meetings.
- Adequate time is dedicated to fulfill partnership objectives.
- The school district brings coherence to improvement efforts.

Appendix B

Collaborative Inquiry as Adaptive Action Guide

Observe: Patterns in Student Learning and Performance
What is the student learning problem that prompts our group's inquiry?
What evidence (patterns in data, observations, student work samples) describes the student learning problem?
Why is this problem important and meaningful to our group?
How is solving this problem related to our school or district priorities?
Our Inquiry Question:

Observe: Patterns of Practice and Organizational Conditions	
Instructional Focus	**Organizational Focus**
What actions have been taken previously to resolve the student learning problem?	*What underlying conditions contribute to the patterns we see:*
What happened? What's working/not working? In what circumstances were previous actions successful? How do we know?	*(1) assumptions about students, student learning, and effective instructional practices we hold and enact individually and collectively?*
What else do we need to know to help us understand the student learning problem and how others have attempted to resolve it?	*(2) agreements about effective instruction and conditions that support learning and teaching?*
	Who else has a stake in or responsibility for resolving the student learning problem?

Based on what we learned through exploring the above questions, do we want to refine our Inquiry Question?

Refined Inquiry Question:

Plan			

What will each of us commit to learn about, try, and share with others in our inquiry group?

When will we take these actions?

What resources (time, information and other data, input from others) will we need?

Action	People Responsible	Timeline	Resources

How will we capture our learning?

How will we know that our actions are on course for improving student learning?

What will we look for as evidence of the impact of our actions on student learning?

What will we look for as evidence of underlying conditions that support learning and teaching?

Act and Reflect	
Instructional Focus	**Organizational Focus**
What happened as we tried new methods? How do we know?	*How has what happened confirmed or challenged the assumptions about students, student learning, and effective instructional practices we hold and enact individually and collectively?*
What patterns of student performance and learning behaviors do we observe?	
	How has what happened confirmed or challenged agreements about effective instruction and conditions that support learning and teaching?
What are we doing differently based on what we learned?	
	How will we share our learning with others beyond our inquiry group?
	How might what we learned inform school or school district priorities?
	How has what happened confirmed or challenged the findings of others?
Further Inquiry	
What questions arose from what we learned?	
What additional information/data do we need to support further inquiry?	

References

Babiera, Rex. (2008). Rowland Unified School District and The Ball Foundation collaborate to improve student literacy achievement. *Review, 8*(1), 1–3.

Babiera, R., & Preskill, H. (2010). *Becoming the change: What one organization working to transform educational systems learned about team learning and change.* Glen Ellyn, IL: The Ball Foundation.

Ball Foundation. (2009). *Ball partnership engagement study.* Ball Foundation Archives, Glen Ellyn, IL.

Ball Foundation. (2010a). *Ball partnership evaluation study.* Ball Foundation Archives, Glen Ellyn, IL.

Ball Foundation. (2010b). *Design principles for organizational learning and capacity building.* Ball Foundation Archives, Glen Ellyn, IL.

Ball Foundation. (2010c). *Framework of competencies for professional practice: Literacy instruction and support for literacy instruction.* Glen Ellyn, IL: Author. Retrieved from http://www.literacyinlearningexchange.org/sites/default/files/ballcomptfr mwkrev2010v.1.pdf

Ball Foundation. (2011). *The Ball-RUSD partnership final evaluation report.* Glen Ellyn, IL: Author.

Ball Foundation. (2012a). Ball Foundation—Human Systems Dynamics Institute collaboration [Interviews]. Ball Foundation Archives, Glen Ellyn, IL.

Ball Foundation. (2012b). *Ball Foundation—Human Systems Dynamics Institute collaboration: Emerging findings from district pilot test.* Ball Foundation Archives, Glen Ellyn, IL.

Ball Foundation. (2012c). *Ball Foundation—Human Systems Dynamics Institute collaboration: Final evaluation report.* Ball Foundation Archives, Glen Ellyn, IL.

Berry, B., Johnson, D., & Montgomery, D. (2005). The power of teacher leadership. *Educational Leadership, 62*(5), 56–60.

Bray, J. N. (2002). Uniting teacher learning: Collaborative inquiry for professional development. *New Directions for Adult and Continuing Education, 94*, 83–92.

Bray, J. N., Lee, J., Smith, L. L., & Yorks, L. (2000). *Collaborative inquiry in practice: Action, reflection, and making meaning.* Thousand Oaks, CA: Sage.

Brooks, A., & Watkins, K. E. (1994). A new era for action technologies: A look at the issues. *New Directions for Adult and Continuing Education, 63,* 5–16.

Brown, J. (with Isaacs, D., & The World Café Community). (2005). *The World Café: Shaping our futures through conversations that matter.* San Francisco: Berrett-Koehler.

Bruce, B. C. (2009). "Building an airplane in the air": The life of the inquiry group. In J. K. Falk & B. Drayton (Eds.), *Creating and sustaining online professional learning communities* (pp. 47–67). New York: Teachers College Press.

Caine, R. N., Caine, G., McClintic, C., & Klimek, K. J. (2009). *12 brain/mind learning principles in action: Developing executive functions of the human brain* (2nd ed.). Thousand Oaks, CA: Corwin Press.

Chrispeels, J. H., & Gonzalez, M. (2006). The challenge of systemic change in complex educational systems: A district model to scale up reform. In A. Harris & J. H. Chrispeels (Eds.), *Improving schools and educational systems: International perspectives* (pp. 241–73). New York: Routledge.

Clark, D. R. (2009). *Fishbowls in learning environments.* Retrieved from: www.nwlink .com/~donclark/hrd/learning/fishbowls.html

Coburn, C. E. (2003). Rethinking scale: Moving beyond numbers to deep and lasting change. *Educational Researcher, 32*(6), 3–12.

Cochran-Smith, M., & Lytle, S. L. (2009). *Inquiry as stance: Practitioner research for the next generation.* New York: Teachers College Press.

Danielson, C. (2007). *Enhancing professional practice: A framework for teaching* (2nd ed.). Alexandria, VA: Association for Supervision and Curriculum Development.

Datnow, A., Hubbard, L., & Mehan, H. (2002). *Extending educational reform: From one school to many.* London: Routledge-Falmer.

Dewey, J. (1933). *How we think: A restatement of the relation of reflective thinking to the educative process.* Lexington, MA: Heath.

DuFour, R. (2004). What is a professional learning community? *Educational Leadership, 61*(8), 6–11.

Duke, D. (2004). *The challenges of educational change.* Boston: Pearson-Allyn and Bacon.

Elementary and Secondary Education Act of 1965, Pub. L. No. 89-10, 79 Stat. 27 (1965).

Elmore, R. F. (1996). Getting to scale with successful educational practice. *Harvard Educational Review, 66*(1), 1–26.

Eoyang, G. H., & Holladay, R. J. (2013). *Adaptive action: Leveraging uncertainty in your organization.* Palo Alto, CA: Stanford University Press.

Fullan, M. (1993). *Change forces: Probing the depth of education reform.* Philadelphia, PA: Falmer Press.

Fullan, M. (2010). *All systems go: The change imperative for whole systems reform.* Thousand Oaks, CA: Corwin Press.

Fullan, M. (2011, October). *Choosing the wrong drivers.* Paper presented at the 15th Annual Conference of the Grantmakers for Education, Los Angeles, CA.

Gallimore, R., Ermeling, B. A., Saunders, W. M., & Goldenberg, C. (2009). Moving the learning of teaching closer to practice: Teacher education implications of school-based inquiry teams. *The Elementary School Journal*, *109*(5), 537–53.

Gilrane, C. P., Roberts, M. L., & Russell, L. A. (2008). Building a community in which everyone teaches, learns, and reads: A case study. *The Journal of Educational Research*, *101*(6): 333–49.

Glennan, T. K., Jr., Bodilly, S. J., Galegher, J. R., & Kerr, K. A. (2004). *Expanding the reach of education reforms: Perspectives from leaders in the scale-up of educational interventions.* Santa Monica, CA: RAND Education. Retrieved from http://www.rand.org/content/dam/rand/pubs/monographs/2004/RAND_MG248.pdf

Holladay, R. (2012, July 19). Building a school district and community mental health services partnership [Email and conversation with author].

Hollins, E. R., McIntyre, L. R., DeBose, C., Hollins, K. S., & Towner, A. (2004). Promoting a self-sustaining learning community: Investigating an internal model for teacher development. *International Journal of Qualitative Studies in Education*, *17*(2), 247–64.

Human Systems Dynamics Institute. (2011). *Adaptive action guide*. Humans Systems Dynamics Institute Archives, Circle Pines, MN.

Iversen, B. (2012, August 13). Adaptive action planning [Email and conversation with author].

King, M. B. (2002). Professional development to promote schoolwide inquiry. *Teaching and Teacher Education, 18*(3), 243–57.

Learning Forward. (2011). *Standards for professional learning*. Oxford, OH: Author.

Lena, C. R. (2011). The missing link in school reform. *Stanford Social Innovation Review, 9*(4), 30–35.

Little, J. W. (2003). Inside teacher community: Representations of classroom practice. *Teachers College Record, 105*(6), 913–45.

McDougall, D., Saunders, W. M., & Goldenberg, C. (2007). Inside the black box of school reform: Explaining the how and why of change at *Getting Results* schools. *International Journal of Disability, Development and Education*, *54*(1), 51–89.

McGill, M. E., Slocum, J. W., Jr., & Lei, D. (1992). Management practices in learning organizations. *Organizational Dynamics, 21*(1), 5–17.

MetLife. (2009). *The MetLife survey of the American teacher: Collaborating for student success.* New York: Author. Retrieved from http://www.eric.ed.gov/PDFS/ED509650.pdf

Mourshed, M., Chijioke, C., Barber, M. (2010). *How the world's most improved school systems keep getting better.* New York: McKinsey Company. Retrieved from http://mckinseyonsociety.com/downloads/reports/Education/How-the-Worlds-Most-Improved-School-Systems-Keep-Getting-Better_Download-version_Final.pdf

National Center for Literacy Education. (2012a). *Asset inventory for collaborative teams.* Urbana, IL: National Center for Literacy Education/National Council of Teachers of English. Retrieved from http://www.literacyinlearningexchange.org/surveys/asset-inventory

National Center for Literacy Education. (2012b). *Building capacity to transform literacy learning*. Urbana, IL: National Center for Literacy Education/National Council of Teachers of English. Retrieved from http://www.literacyinlearningexchange.org/sites/default/files/ncleshortlitreview.pdf

National Center for Literacy Education. (2012c). *Capacity building continua*. Urbana, IL: National Center for Literacy Education/National Council of Teachers of English. Retrieved from http://www.literacyinlearningexchange.org/sites/default/files/continuaforcapacitybuilding.pdf

National Center for Literacy Education. (2012d). *Framework for capacity building: Conditions and practices that support effective collaboration*. Urbana, IL: National Center for Literacy Education/National Council of Teachers of English. Retrieved from http://www.literacyinlearningexchange.org/page/framework-capacity-building

National Center for Literacy Education. (2013). *Remodeling literacy learning: Making room for what works*. Urbana, IL: National Center for Literacy Education/National Council of Teachers of English. Retrieved from http://www.literacyinlearningexchange.org/remodeling

National Governors Association Center for Best Practices, Council of Chief State School Officers. (2010). *Common Cores State Standards*. Washington, DC: Authors.

Nelson, T., & Slavit, D. (2008). Supported teacher collaborative inquiry. *Teacher Education Quarterly, 35*(1), 99–116.

No Child Left Behind Act of 2001, Pub. L. No. 107-110, 115 Stat. 1425 (2002). Retrieved from http://www2.ed.gov/policy/elsec/leg/esea02/107-110.pdf

Owen, H. (2007). Open space technology. In P. Holman, T. Devane, & S. Cady (Eds.), *The change handbook: The definitive resource on today's best methods for engaging whole systems* (pp.135–48). San Francisco: Berrett-Koehler.

Parsons, B. (2009). Evaluative inquiry for complex times. *OD Practitioner, 41*(1), 44–49.

Patterson, L. (2012, July 31). Adaptive action at North Star of Texas Writing Project [Email and conversation with author].

Patterson, L., Wickstrom, C., Roberts, J., Araujo, J., & Hoki, C. (2010). Deciding when to step in and when to back off: Culturally mediated writing instruction for adolescent English learners. *The Tapestry Journal, 2*(1), 1–18. Retrieved from http://tapestry.usf.edu/journal/documents/v01n02%20-%20MS%231-Patterson_Culturally%20Med%20Writing.pdf

Phillips, J. (2003). Powerful learning: Creating learning communities in urban school reform. *Journal of Curriculum and Supervision, 18*(3), 240–58.

Rafferty, C. D. (1995, February). *Impact and challenges of multi-site collaborative inquiry initiatives*. Paper presented at the Annual Meeting of the American Association of Colleges for Teacher Education, Washington, DC.

Rowland Unified School District. (2008). *Strategic plan*. Retrieved from http://www.rowlandschools.org/ourpages/auto/2008/2/7/1202419082334/RUSDStrategicPlanMissionBeliefs.pdf

Rowland Unified School District. (2011). *Framework for efficacious instruction*. Rowland Heights, CA: Author.

Sagor, R. (2000). *Guiding school improvement with action research*. Alexandria, VA: Association for Supervision and Curriculum Development.

Sander, M. A., Everts, J., & Johnson, J. (2011). Using data to inform program design and implementation and make the case for school mental health. *Advances in School Mental Health Promotion, 4*(4), 13–21.

Senge, P. M. (1990). The fifth discipline: The art and practice of the learning organization. New York: Currency Doubleday.

Serrat, O. (2009, December). *A primer on organizational learning* (Knowledge Solutions Series No. 69). Manila, Philippines: Asian Development Bank. Retrieved from http://www.adb.org/sites/default/files/pub/2009/primer-on-organizational-learning.pdf

Stoll, L., Bolam, R., McMahon, A., Wallace, M., & Thomas, S. (2006). Professional learning communities: A review of the literature. *Journal of Educational Change, 7*(4), 221–58.

Strahan, D. (2003). Promoting a collaborative professional culture in three elementary schools that have beaten the odds. *The Elementary School Journal, 104*(2), 127–46.

Stringer, E. T. (2007). *Action research* (3rd ed.). Thousand Oaks, CA: Sage.

Supovitz, J. A. (2002). Developing communities of instructional practice. *Teachers College Record, 104*(8), 1591–626.

Supovitz, J. A., & Christman, J. B. (2003). *Developing communities of instructional practice: Lessons for Cincinnati and Philadelphia* (CPRE Policy Briefs No. RB-39). Philadelphia: Consortium for Policy Research in Education, University of Pennsylvania.

Talbert, J. E., & McLaughlin, M. W. (2002). Professional communities and the artisan model of teaching. *Teachers and Teaching: Theory and Practice, 8*(3/4), 325–43.

Teachers College. (2010). Teachers College Reading and Writing Project. Retrieved from http://readingandwritingproject.com/

Thibodeau, G. M. (2008). A content literacy collaborative study group: High school teachers take charge of their professional learning. *Journal of Adolescent and Adult Literacy, 52*(1), 54–64.

Thompson, S. C., Gregg, L., & Niska, J. M. (2004). Professional learning communities, leadership, and student learning. *Research in Middle Level Education Online, 28*(1), 1–15.

Timperley, H. S., & Parr, J. M. (2007). Closing the achievement gap through evidence-based inquiry at multiple levels of the education system. *Journal of Advanced Academics, 19*(1), 90–115.

Tyack, D. B., & Cuban, L. (1995). *Tinkering toward utopia: A century of public school reform*. Cambridge, MA: Harvard University Press.

Tytel, M., & Holladay, R. (2011). *Simple rules: A radical inquiry into self*. Apache Junction, AZ: Gold Canyon Press.

Vescio, V., Ross, D., & Adams, A. (2006, January). *A review of research on professional learning communities: What do we know?* Paper presented at the National School Reform Faculty (NSRF) Research Forum, Denver, CO.

Wylie, E. C., Lyon, C. J., & Goe, L. (2009). *Teacher professional development focused on formative assessment: Changing teachers, changing schools* (ETS Research Rep. No. RR-09-10). Princeton, NJ: Educational Testing Service.

Zech, L. K., Gause-Vega, C. L., Bray, M. H., Secules, T., & Goldman, S.R. (2000). Content-based collaborative inquiry: A professional development model for sustaining educational reform. *Educational Psychologist, 35*(3), 207–17.

Index

Danielson, Charlotte, 35
data and evidence
    collaborative inquiry and, 22, 24*t*, 68*t*
    professional learning and, 16
    student learning and, 44, 45*f*
decision making, 49–50
deprivatizing practice, 44, 45*f*
depth, 5
Dewey, John, 10, 11, 66
district-wide capacity building. *See* system-wide learning and capacity building

Education Initiatives (EI) team, Ball Foundation, 28–36, 59, 61
education reform. *See* reform efforts, large-scale; traditional approach to education reform
Elementary and Secondary Education Act (1965), 11
elementary schools
    improved overall achievement, 18
    instructional practice at, 14
    shared practice and, 20
    targeted students, improved achievement for, 19
Elmore, Richard, 2, 4, 6, 66, 70
Eoyang, Glenda, 54, 60
evidence. *See* data and evidence
expertise and perspectives of others, seeking, 21–22, 24*t*, 68*t*

faculty meetings, 16
Fifth Discipline, The (Senge), 28
focus, 15, 17
Ford Foundation, 6
"Framework for Capacity Building" (NCLE), 44–46, 45*f*
"Framework for Efficacious Instruction" (Rowland Unified School District), 35–36, 37, 38, 39, 49
"Framework of Competencies for Professional Practice" (Ball Foundation), 40–41, 42*f*
Fullan, Michael, xiii, 3, 6, 70

Gonzalez, Margarita, 7–8

high schools. *See* secondary schools
Holladay, Royce, 51, 56, 57–58
human systems dynamics, 53–55
Human Systems Dynamics Institute (HSDI), 53–54, 61

Human Systems Dynamics Institute Network, 57

infrastructure and organizational support
    broad, inclusive, and coherent, 7
    collaborative inquiry, supporting, 41–43
    for collaborative professional learning and practice, 46–50, 47*t*
    competencies to provide and support literary instruction, 41, 42*f*
    educator roles, premise of, 40–41
    isolated vs. collaborative practice and, 43–44
    NCLE domains and framework, 44–46, 45*f*
    professional learning and, 16–17
    taking Ball Foundation approach to scale, 50–51, 51*f*
inquiry, collaborative. *See also* professional learning and development, collaborative inquiry-based; system-wide learning and capacity building
    as adaptive action, 64–66, 67*f*, 75*f*–78*f*
    defined, xiii–xiv
    history of professional learning and, 10–12
    instructional practice, impact on, 14–16
    key elements of, 19–23, 24*t*, 27
    leadership practice, impact on, 16
    mindset or stance of, 29*t*, 38, 44, 45*f*, 48, 63–64
    norms of practice for, 41, 43
    organizational conditions, effects on, 16–17
    other approaches distinguished from, 23–25
    spillover of, 48
    structural supports for, 43
    student result findings, 17–19
    studies (overview), 12–13
inside-out perspective, 31
instructional practice. *See also* literacy learning and instruction
    coherence in, 17
    collaborative inquiry, impact of, 14–16
    district-wide agreements for effective instruction, 35–36
    educator roles to provide or support, 40–41
    planning, action, and reflection cycles, 22, 24*t*

Author

Michael J. Palmisano has served as an elementary and middle school teacher, school and district administrator, and (adjunct) university faculty member. Most recently, he worked with a team of consultants supported by the Ball Foundation in Glen Ellyn, Illinois, in partnering with mid-size urban school districts to improve student literacy through a collaborative and system-wide capacity-building approach. His current work as an education consultant enacts his commitment to improving instruction, leadership, and organizational practices in schools and school districts through educators coming together to learn with and from one another to build their capacity to adapt, innovate, and respond to meet the needs of students in their settings. In addition to developing resources to support collaborative inquiry approaches

to organizational learning and system-wide change in education, Palmisano has authored publications for school and district improvement and accreditation. In 1994, he was invited by the Illinois State Board of Education to lead the Illinois Learning Standards Project and to serve as an advisor as the agency evolved to support standards-based education reform. Palmisano is a former president of Illinois ASCD and a former member of the ASCD Board of Directors.

This book was typeset in TheMix and Palatino by Barbara Frazier.

Typefaces used on the cover include Trajan Pro and Galaxie Polaris Condensed–Medium.

The book was printed on 50-lb. Opaque Offset paper by Versa Press, Inc.